S0-BCZ-039

FAITHFUL FRIENDSHIP

BY DOROTHY C. DEVERS

"Hail Guest! We ask not what thou art:
If Friend, we greet thee, hand and heart:
If Stranger, such no longer be:
If Foe, our love shall conquer thee." *

* Author unknown. From Patriotic Poems America Loves, compiled by Jean Anne Vincent. Copyright Doubleday & Company, Inc., Garden City, N.Y. 1968.

Christian Growth and Spiritual Direction

through

FAITHFUL FRIENDSHIP

Dorothy C. Devers
of the
Faithful Friends Mission Group
The Church of The Saviour
Washington, D. C.

A Forward Movement Miniature Book

To Mimi — the "rare treasure"

through whom a cherished theory

became a living truth

BV
4647
.F7
D4
1980

Excerpts from the Revised Standard Version of the Bible copyrighted 1946, 1952
(c) 1971, 1973.

Excerpts from The Jerusalem Bible, copyright (c) 1966 by Darton, Longman &
Todd, Ltd. and Doubleday & Company, Inc. Used by permission of the publisher.

Privately printed by the author, 1979. Reprinted 1980 by Forward Movement
Publications, 412 Sycamore Street, Cincinnati, Ohio 45202.

CONTENTS

Grateful acknowledgment is made to the authors, copyright holders, and publishers of articles and books from which reprints serve as pertinent study
materials. Proper acknowledgment is made on each page of reprints.

CONTENTS (continued)

CONTENTS (continued)

PURPOSE AND PLAN OF HANDBOOK

The need for trusting relationships is universal and urgent. The need for love and joy and peace between and among persons as individuals, as members of groups, classes, races and nations is everywhere evident.

This little book suggests a disciplined Way

—to grow

—to receive and to give direction
in the life of the spirit
through one-to-one relationship, and

—to understand what it is to be "faithful
friend" in every relationship of life

with the help of Him Who is Faithful Friend to each one of us.

This plan is in twelve parts, each part intended to cover one week, including definite structure, suggestions for meditation on Scripture as the gateway to prayer, and accompanying pages for pertinent study.

The format of this handbook was planned so that its pages will fit into any standard three-ring binder that accommodates 8½" x 5½" sheets. Standard fillers 8½" x 5½" can be purchased and pages inserted for personal journal and for returned accountability reports. (See The Keeping of a Journal, paragraph 1, page 17.)

Any two persons seriously desirous of growing in the life of the spirit, and committed to following a disciplined Way, will find this small book a spur, a guide, and a kind of launching pad from which their spirits will continue to soar in their own unique ways.

USE OF HANDBOOK — BY INDIVIDUALS, GROUPS, AND CONGREGATIONS

The twelve-week plan of suggested procedure to encourage Christian growth and spiritual direction through one-to-one relationship may be used in various ways and in different contexts. For example, it may be used by:

One Christian seeking spiritual growth through companionship with another.

"A faithful friend is the elixir of life
and those who fear the Lord will find one . . . "
(Ecclesiasticus 6:16 Jer.)
(fear meaning also "hold in awe" or "revere").

You may yearn to grow in the life of the spirit without ever crediting any of your associates with having a similar desire. But if God has implanted a yearning for himself in every heart—that yearning in another's heart is your secret ally. Pray for the capacity to see it, and then watch for an expression of that ally at home, among the members of your family; at work, among your colleagues; at school, among classmates; at play, among close or casual friends; at church, among the members of your group or community; or when you happen to meet someone at a time and place that seem to be sheer "coincidence." You may find that ally where and when you least expect to. Be ready to greet and to give to that person "the reason for the hope that is in you." Stretch out your hand—and you may be surprised how eagerly and how firmly it is grasped by a potential faithful friend.

Such a relationship may last for a short time or for a life-time. In either case it will, if taken seriously, have eternally significant consequences, for, once having had and having been a faithful friend, you will find every relationship improved and influenced by the experience.

Members of a group who want to be more than "nominal Christians."

A determination can be made to divide off by two's (one set of three's if the number be uneven) in order to experience the twelve-week process. The periodic meetings of the entire group should include times of corporate silence, meditation on the Scriptures and study pages for that week, followed by sharing of evaluations of what is happening in and among the members.

USE OF HANDBOOK (continued)

At the end of twelve weeks, if earnest effort and time have been devoted, the faithful friends of the group will be fired with unpredictable inspiration and purpose, for their gifts will have been discerned and their zeal will have been aroused. New thrusts of mission, individual and corporate, may issue as the friends enthusiastically seek to exercise their gifts in furtherance of the work of the Kingdom.

Members of a Christian group with a corporate focus or mission have a primary commitment to Jesus Christ, are committed to the mission for his sake, and to one another whose mutual Friend he is.

In such a group every person should be willing to be paired off with any other person as "faithful friend" not only to learn the process but to deepen a relationship with any one member of the group—for Christ's sake, and for the sake of the mission.

At the end of the twelve-week period, a rotation could be made so that a relationship with another group member could be deepened. The essential disciplines would be maintained, but pertinent new study materials having to do with Christian growth, spiritual direction, and mission, would be determined by the members of the group.

In a group with a corporate task, rotation of "faithful friends" enables each person to know and love better each other person—and thus the gifts of each one are discerned, the bonds are strengthened, and the mission prospers.

Members of a congregation or parish who may sit in a pew, Sunday after Sunday, feeling isolated from their fellow-members, wistfully wishing there were someone with whom to talk about prayer or God or faith or pain or anxiety. Such a pity that they cannot 'find' one another when one soul can so readily "set another on fire." If just two of them could be brought together and offered a structure to encourage their meditation, prayer, and sharing—their lives could be changed, their energies focussed, Christ's love experienced, and his work expanded. One such relationship in a congregation could be a powerful leaven for lifting up the whole body.

FAITHFUL FRIENDSHIP — THE GREAT ENTERPRISE

In a book entitled The Great Enterprise, published in 1952, H.A. Overstreet wrote: "The most needed enterprise of our age is to discover how to create such environments that the generous and constructive pattern of personality—one that relates itself affirmatively to all its fellows—will become the predominating pattern of our culture." * That sounds like a psychiatrist's adaptation of something that was said two thousand years ago: "Thou shalt love thy neighbor as thyself."

Bernard Häring's definition of prayer offers a clue to the means of carrying out the great enterprise; "Prayer is joyous acceptance of life's greatest gift, the Lord's friendship, and the return of the gift of one's self to God in the service of one's fellowmen." * *

How do we encourage others first to accept the Lord's friendship and then, in turn, to become capable of bestowing his kind of friendship on others? How, in fact, do I do this myself? In other words— where and how are men to find spiritual direction? How do we Christians endeavor to provide spiritual direction to modern man? How, indeed, do we find spiritual direction ourselves?

One strong feature of The Church of The Saviour in Washington, D.C., is emphasis on deepening the life of prayer through acceptance by its members of disciplines of daily meditation and prayer. Years ago, having practiced these disciplines, we became aware of our need of spiritual direction. Our first thought was to look outside the community for one-to-one direction from great spirits whom we had learned to love and respect. Somehow this never worked out. A very few of us found our direction through the books of von Hugel, Underhill, St. Ignatius, St. John of the Cross, St. Francis de Sales, Caussade, Douglas Steere, John Coburn, Grou, and others—which we perused with care and whose admonitions we endeavored to follow. Some of us firmly believe that he who truly seeks a director will find one—that that much-needed and to-become-cherished book does not fall into one's hands by sheer chance.

---

* Copyright, 1952, by W. W. Norton & Company, Inc., p. 140.

* * Bernard Häring, Prayer: The Integration of Faith and Life. Copyright (c) 1975: Fides Publishers, Inc., Notre Dame, Indiana 46556, p. 1.

FAITHFUL FRIENDSHIP — THE GREAT ENTERPRISE (continued)

Some years ago, at a time when there were twelve members in the Retreat Mission Group of The Church of The Saviour, I was designated spiritual director. I found myself incapable of relating to twelve persons simultaneously in any kind of depth. Even to read and respond with any degree of careful concern to twelve accountability reports each week was impossible. It was then that I came alive with a hope for a new way to encourage spiritual growth—and perhaps even to develop what Steere calls "a much more tentative type of spiritual guidance."

If the "greatest pastoral need is spiritual direction"—and if we don't have spiritual directors in the classic sense—we do the best we can with the resources we have. "Better to light one candle than to curse the dark." And, perhaps, in the process, we, by the grace of God, produce a few embryo spiritual directors.

In an article written by Douglas Steere in 1965 on spiritual direction he said, "Such types of spiritual direction as we have in Protestantism have often come in . . . informal . . . contexts: from prayer groups and confraternities; from two laymen conferring together on their common need; and from pastor to laymen in highly empirical fashion as between two friends engaged in a common quest."

Then I remembered that St. Francis de Sales refers to the spiritual guide as a 'faithful friend' and quotes Ecclesiasticus 6: 14, 16. Of course, St. Francis goes on to say that St. Teresa of Avila advised, "For this purpose choose one out of a thousand . . . " St. Francis goes her one better: "For my part, I say one out of ten thousand, for there are fewer men than we realize who are capable of this task." But then, more encouraging, he says hopefully, "Who shall find such a friend? The Wise Man answers, 'Those who fear the Lord,' that is, humble souls who sincerely desire to make spiritual progress." *

How, then, to act upon this promise in down-to-earth fashion? If Caussade's words, "God still speaks to us today as he spoke to our fathers," be true—how best to listen to the Word of God—how learn from him? Certainly through prayer which is 'response to the Lord's friendship,' for the Lord is a Faithful Friend, always with us to direct us, and telling us, "Even as the Father sent me, so I send you" to be faithful friends.

---

* St. Francis de Sales, Introduction to the Devout Life, translated, with an Introduction and Notes, by John K. Ryan. Copyright (c) 1950, 1952, 1966 by John K. Ryan. Image Books, a Division of Doubleday & Company, Inc., Garden City, New York, p. 46-47.

FAITHFUL FRIENDSHIP — THE GREAT ENTERPRISE (continued)

My looseleaf notebook concerning faithful friendship began to take shape—gleanings from the Scriptures, the saints, great spiritual directors, psychologists, theologians, philosophers—with the quote from Ecclesiasticus as the frontispiece:

"A faithful friend is a sure shelter,
    Whoever finds one has found a rare treasure.
A faithful friend is something beyond price,
    there is no measuring his worth.
A faithful friend is the elixir of life,
    and those who fear the Lord will find one.
Whoever fears the Lord makes true friends,
    for as a man is, so is his friend."

(Ecclesiasticus 6: 14-17 Jer.)

(Last line above is usually interpreted:
    'for his friend is as dear to him as himself'—
but equally probable is:
    'for his friend will be inevitably like
himself, God-fearing.')

(From note f in Jerusalem Bible)

Comparatively few persons today recognize their need for a spiritual director. But almost everyone knows his need for a faithful friend. St. Francis says a spiritual director is a faithful friend. It seemed reasonable to me to try to encourage the members of my group to become faithful friends to one another—ever leaning on the promise of the ever-present spirit of Christ where two or three are gathered together in his name—in the hope that some sound mutual spiritual direction might result. Something John Coburn said encouraged me: "The spiritual director need not take himself too seriously. God is going to get his work done if he is taken seriously."

Now, despite the fact that I am well aware that "we come to God by love and not by navigation," I tried a bit of navigation—and devised a structure. (If "we come to God by love,"—what about "we come to love by God"?) With the promise of Christ, the Wonderful Counselor, that he will abide in and with us; with the assurance from him that what he did we can do, assurance from him who 'knew what was in man'—we Christians can be expectant in a special way as we engage in the disciplines of faithful friendship.

FAITHFUL FRIENDSHIP — THE GREAT ENTERPRISE (continued)

The pages for study in each assignment have been selected with care, as have the accompanying Scriptures for daily meditation. We supplement our study materials and share with our friend anything from our own reading or writing that we consider helpful to:

1. Encourage us to hear and obey the Word of God.

2. Enable us to say "fiat mihi" and to mean it.

3. Recognize Jesus Christ as Faithful Friend and, in turn, to "be kind to one another, tender-hearted, forgiving one another— to walk in love, as Christ loved us and gave himself up for us."

We exchange autobiographies. We keep journals. We learn to listen—to listen in prayer, to listen to another, practicing being truly 'present.' We learn to grow through communicating with another. We are enabled to develop certain attributes—humility, trusting attitude, capacity to love. Our daily life is the laboratory where we test and practice what we have studied and pondered in our daily quiet time and in our times with our faithful friend.

In accepting the challenge of the great enterprise, our endeavor is three-fold:

1. We commit ourselves to enter into a more intimate relationship with Jesus Christ than we have ever before enjoyed.

All of life is relationship—relationship with God the Father through his son, Jesus Christ; relationship with self; relationship with others; relationship with material things; and relationship with events and circumstances. Relationship with God through Jesus Christ is the most important for it governs all other relationships. Therefore, we will endeavor to steep ourselves in meditation on Jesus Christ—we will endeavor to make such meditation a growing and strengthening habit, a habit which will ever be an essential part of life.

Because "the world is so much with us," few of us who profess to be Christians consistently experience the peace, confidence, and strength that in our quiet moments we sometimes know. For that rare person who is truly aware that Jesus Christ is his ever-present friend—life is totally different from the life of one who is unaware of his presence.

FAITHFUL FRIENDSHIP — THE GREAT ENTERPRISE (continued)

The practice of faithful friendship requires commitment to concrete, down-to-earth, hour-by-hour and moment-by-moment activity. We are not engaging in child's play, although our aim is to be childlike. We are not giving lip-service to some idealistic fantasy. Instead, we are setting out on the path near at hand, among the familiar persons and in the places where we live our daily lives, with light for one step at a time, but with firm determination to take that step so that the light and the strength for the next one will be forthcoming.

2. We purposely endeavor to become a faithful friend to one other depending on Jesus Christ who is Faithful Friend to each of us.

In this endeavor we are being present to, praying for and with our friend; listening for and to him/her; discerning what he would say if he could articulate all he feels; comforting him; confronting him when confrontation is called for; requiring of him and giving to him accountability. Thus does one strengthen the other, help him to grow spiritually, pick him up when he falls down, support him, trust and encourage him, foster hope in him—and in turn is comforted, confronted, and strengthened by the other. To be a faithful friend in this humble, helpful way is to give and to receive spiritual direction. We do what we can with what we have where we are in the moment—with the help of God.

3. Earnest endeavor to fulfill Paragraphs 1 and 2 above prepares us to live among all our associates—from the intimate members of our immediate family to the persons we meet only fleetingly—in a more and more affirmative manner, more and more in the Spirit of Christ. "As the Father sent me, so I am sending you." (John 20:21. Jer.)

Thus do we meet the challenge of the great enterprise and fulfill the command to love God and neighbor.

No. 1 — HAVING THE FAITHFUL FRIEND

A. Adventure in Meditation: The Source of life—and I.

All knowledge of the world, with the exception of one item, has come to me through the gateway of my five senses—seeing, hearing, tasting, smelling, touching. But suppose, through accident or illness, I were deprived of my senses and lay in bed blind, deaf, dumb, unable to smell or to feel. Someone dear to me might bend over me, touch me, and speak tender words of comfort, but I would be completely unaware—absolutely cut off from the outward world. I would have only one indisputable fact of immediate knowledge, as distinct from memory: self-consciousness, self-awareness—the one exception to which reference was made above.* I would know myself to be a living being and could silently say: "I am."

"Consideration" is another word for meditation. Let us consider this fascinating and tremendous mystery: the breath of life, the spark of life, the ability I have to say "I am" because of Him whose name is I AM.

— "Say . . . I AM has sent me to you." (Exodus 3: 11-14, especially vs. 14 RSV)

— "Let us make man in our image." (Gen. 1: 26-27 RSV)

— "God . . . breathed into his nostrils the breath of life, and man became a living being." (Gen. 2: 7 RSV)

— ". . . before Abraham was, I am." (John 8:58 RSV)

— "I am the true vine . . . " (John 15: 1-11 RSV)

— " . . . that they may all be one; even as thou, Father, art in me, and I in thee . . . that they may be one even as we are one. I in them, and thou in me, that they may become perfectly one . . . that the love with which thou hast loved me may be in them, and I in them." (John 17:21-22, 26)

B. Read: — The Higher Friendship
— The Father is Very Fond of Me } see following pages

C. Make a list and place it in your folder of those persons with whom your relationship is: good, fair, strained, neglected, very poor.

D. Write: a brief spiritual autobiography (just one or two pages) to give to your "faithful friend," recalling those times when, in retrospect, God's hand seemed to have been on your shoulder.

* Adapted from The Use of Silence by Geoffrey Hoyland, Inner life Series No. 5, London S.P.C.K. 1955.

THE HIGHER FRIENDSHIP *

The solitude of life in its ultimate issue is because we were made for a higher companionship. It is just in the innermost sanctuary, shut to every other visitant, that God meets us. We are driven to God by the needs of the heart. If the existence of God was due to a purely intellectual necessity; if we believed in Him only because our reason gave warrant for the faith; it would not matter much whether He really is, and whether we really can know Him. But when the instincts of our nature, and the necessities of the heart-life demand God, we are forced to believe. In moments of deep feeling, when all pretence is silenced, a man may be still able to question the existence of God, but he does not question his own need of God. Man, to remain man, must believe in the possibility of this relationship with the divine. There is a love which passeth the love of women, passeth the love of comrades, passeth all earthly love, the love of God to the weary, starved heart of man.

To believe in this great fact does not detract from human friendship, but really gives it worth and glory. It is because of this, that all love has a place in the life of man. All our worships, and friendships, and loves, come from God, and are but reflections of the divine tenderness. All that is beautiful, and lovely and pure, and of good repute, finds its appropriate setting in God; for it was made by God. He made it for Himself. He made man with instincts, and aspirations, and heart-hunger, and divine unrest, that He might give them full satisfaction in Himself. He claims everything, but He gives everything. Our human relationships are sanctified and glorified by the spiritual union. He gives us back our kinships, and friendships, with a new light on them, an added tenderness, transfiguring our common ties and intimacies, flooding them with a supernal joy. We part from men to meet with God, that we may be able to meet men again on a higher platform. But the love of God is the end and design of all other loves. If the flowers and leaves fade, it is that the time of ripe fruit is at hand . . . We may have tasted of all the joys the world can offer, have known success and the gains of success, been blessed with the sweetest friendships and the fiercest loves; but if we have not found this the chief end of life, we have missed our chance, and can only have at the last a desolated life.

But if through the joy or through the sorrow of life, through love or the want of it, through the gaining of friends or the loss of them, we have been led to dower our lives with the friendship of God, we

---

* Hugh Black. Friendship, Copyright, 1898, by Fleming H. Revell Company. Reprinted by permission of the publisher. Pp. 219-237.

THE HIGHER FRIENDSHIP * (continued)

are possessed of the incorruptible, and undefiled and that passeth not away . . .

. . . the root of all religion is this mystical union, a communion with the Unseen, a friendship with God open to man. Religion is not an acceptance of a creed, or a burden of commandments, but a personal secret of the soul, to be attained each man for himself. It is the experience of the nearness of God, the mysterious contact with the divine, and the consciousness that we stand in a special individual relationship with Him. The first state of exaltation, when the knowledge burst upon the soul, cannot, of course, last; but its effect remains in inward peace, and outward impulse toward nobler life.

Men of all ages have known this close relationship. The possibility of it is the glory of life: the fact of it is the romance of history, and the true reading of history. All devout men that have ever lived have lived in the light of this communion. All religious experience has had this in common, that somehow the soul is so possessed by God, that doubt of His existence ceases; and the task of life becomes to keep step with Him, so that there may be correspondence between the outer and the inner conditions of life. Men have known this communion in such a degree that they have been called preeminently the Friends of God, but something of the experience which underlies the term is true of the pious of all generations.

To us, in our place in history, communion with God comes through Jesus Christ. It is an ineffable mystery, but it is still a fact of experience. Only through Jesus do we know God, His interest in us, His desire for us, His purpose with us. He not only shows us in His own example the blessedness of a life in fellowship with the Father, but He makes it possible for us. United to Jesus, we know ourselves united to God. The power of Jesus is not limited to the historical impression made by His life. It entered the world as history; it lives in the world as spiritual fact today. Luther's experience is the experience of all believers, "To me it is not simply an old story of an event that happened once; for it is a gift, a bestowing, that endures forever." We offer Christ the submission of our hearts, and the obedience of our lives; and He offers us His abiding presence. We take Him as our Master; and He takes us as His friends. "I call you no longer servants," He said to His disciples, "but I have called you friends." The servant knoweth not what his Master doeth, his only duty is to obey; a friend is admitted to confidence, and though he may do the same thing as a servant, he does not do it any longer unreasoningly, but, having been taken into counsel, he knows why he is doing it. This was Christ's method with His disciples, not to

---

* Hugh Black. Friendship, Copyright, 1898, by Fleming H. Revell Company. Reprinted by permission of the publisher. Pp. 219-237.

THE HIGHER FRIENDSHIP * (continued)

apportion to each his task, but to show them His great purpose for the world, and to ask for their service and devotion to carry it out.

The distinction is not that a servant pleases his master, and a friend pleases himself. It is that our Lord takes us up into a relationship of love with Himself, and we go out into life inspired with His spirit to work His work. It begins with the self-surrender of love; and love, not fear nor favor, becomes the motive. To feel thus the touch of God on our lives changes the world. Its fruits are joy, and peace, and confidence that all the events of life are suffused, not only with meaning, but with a meaning of love. The higher friendship brings a satisfaction of the heart, and a joy commensurate to the love. Its reward is itself, the sweet, enthralling relationship, not any adventitious gain it promises, either in the present, or for the future. Even if there were no physical, or moral, rewards and punishments in the world, we would still love and serve Christ for His own sake. The soul that is bound by this personal attachment to Jesus has a life in the eternal, which transfigures the life in time with a great joy.

We can see at once that to be the friend of God will mean peace also. It has brought peace over the troubled lives of all His friends throughout the ages. Every man who enters into the covenant, knows the world to be a spiritual arena, in which the love of God manifests itself. He walks no longer on a sodden earth and under a grey sky; for he knows that, though all men misunderstand him, he is understood, and followed with loving sympathy, in heaven. It was this confidence in God as a real and near friend, which gave to Abraham's life such distinction, and the calm repose which made his character so impressive. Strong in the sense of God's friendship, he lived above the world, prodigal of present possessions, because sure of the future, waiting securely in the hope of the great salvation. He walked with God in sweet unaffected piety, and serene faith, letting his character ripen in the sunshine, and living out his life as unto God not unto men. To know the love of God does not mean the impoverishing of our lives, by robbing them of their other sweet relations. Rather, it means the enriching of these, by revealing their true beauty and purpose. Sometimes we are brought nearer God through our friends, if not through their influence or the joy of their love, then through the discipline which comes from their very limitations and from their loss. But oftener the experience has been that, through our union with the Friend of friends, we are led into richer and fuller intercourse with our fellows. The nearer we get to the centre of the circle, the nearer we get to each other. To be joined together in Christ

---

* Hugh Black. Friendship, Copyright, 1898, by Fleming H. Revell Company. Reprinted by permission of the publisher. Pp. 219-237.

THE HIGHER FRIENDSHIP * (continued)

is the only permanent union, deeper than the tie of blood, higher than the bond of kin, closer than the most sacred earthly relationship. Spiritual kinship is the great nexus to unite men. "Who are My brethren?" asked Jesus, and for answer pointed to His disciples, and added, "Whosoever shall do the will of My Father in heaven the same is My mother and sister and brother."

We ought to make more of our Christian friendships, the communion of the saints, the fellowship of believers. "They that feared God spake often one with the other," said the prophet Malachi in one of the darkest hours of the church. What mutual comfort, and renewed hope, they would get from, and give to, each other! Faith can be increased, and love stimulated, and enthusiasm revived by intercourse. The supreme friendship with Christ therefore will not take from us any of our treasured intimacies, unless they are evil. It will increase the number of them, and the true force of them. It will link us on to all who love the same Lord in sincerity and truth. It will open our heart to the world of men that Jesus loved and gave His life to save.

This friendship with the Lord knows no fear of loss; neither life, nor death, nor things present, nor things to come can separate us. It is joy and strength in the present, and it lights up the future with a great hope. We are not much concerned about speculations regarding the future; for we know that we are in the hands of our Lover. All that we care to assert of the future is, that Christ will in an ever fuller degree be the environment of all Christian souls, and the effect of that constant environment will fulfill the aspiration of the apostle, "We shall be like Him, for we shall see Him as He is." Communion produces likeness. This even now is the test of our friendship with the Lord. Are we assimilating His mind, His way of looking at things, His judgments, His spirit? Is the Christ-conscience being developed in us? Have we an increasing interest in the things which interest Him, an increasing love of the things that He loves, an increasing desire to serve the purpose He has at heart? "Ye are My friends if ye do whatsoever I command you," is the test by which we can try ourselves.

Fellowship with Him, being much in His company, thinking of Him, seeking to please Him, will produce likeness, and bring us together on more intimate terms. For, as love leads to the desire for fuller fellowship, so fellowship leads to a deeper love. Even if sometimes we almost doubt whether we are really in this blessed covenant of friendship, our policy is to go on loving Him, serving Him, striving

---

* Hugh Black. Friendship, Copyright, 1898, by Fleming H. Revell Company. Reprinted by permission of the publisher. Pp. 219-237.

THE HIGHER FRIENDSHIP * (continued)

to please Him; and we will yet receive assurance, which will bring peace; He will not disappoint us at the last. It is worth all the care and effort we can give, to have and to keep Him for our friend who will be a lasting possession, whose life enters into the very fibre of our life, and whose love makes us certain of God.

We ought to use our faith in this friendship to bless our lives. To have an earthly friend, whom we trust and reverence, can be to us a source of strength, keeping us from evil, making us ashamed of evil. The dearer the friend and the more spiritual the friendship, the keener will be this feeling, and the more needful does it seem to keep the garments clean. It must reach its height of intensity and of moral effectiveness in the case of friendship with God. There can be no motive on earth so powerful. If we could only have such a friendship, we see at once what an influence it might have over our life. We can appreciate more than the joy, and peace, and comfort of it; we can feel the power of it. To know ourselves ever before a living, loving Presence, having a constant sense of Christ abiding in us, taking Him with us into the marketplace, into our business and our pleasure, to have Him as our familiar friend in joy and sorrow, in gain and loss, in success and failure, must, in accordance with all psychological law, be a source of strength, lifting life to a higher level of thought, and feeling, and action. Supposing it were true and possible, it would naturally be the strongest force in the world, the most effective motive that could be devised; it would affect the whole moral outlook, and make some things easy now deemed impossible, and make some things impossible now to our shame too easy. Supposing this covenant with God were true, and we knew ourselves to have such a Lover of our soul, it would, as a matter of course, give us deeper and more serious views of human life, and yet take away from us the burden and the unrest of life.

. . . Christ's work on earth was to make the friendship of God possible to all. It seems too good to be true, too wondrous a condescension on His part, but its reality has been tested, and attested, by generations of believers. This covenant of friendship is open to us, to be ours in life, and in death, and past the gates of death.

The human means of communication is prayer, though we limit it sadly. Prayer is not an act of worship merely, the bending of the knee on set occasions, and offering petitions in need. It is an attitude of soul, opening the life on the Godward side, and keeping free communication with the world of spirit. And so, it is possible to pray always, and to keep our friendship ever green and sweet: and God comes back upon the life, as dew upon the thirsty ground. There is

* Hugh Black. Friendship, Copyright, 1898, by Fleming H. Revell Company. Reprinted by permission of the publisher. Pp. 219-237.

THE HIGHER FRIENDSHIP * (continued)

an interchange of feeling, a responsiveness of love, a thrill of mutual friendship.

> "You must love Him, ere to you
> He shall seem worthy of your love."

The great appeal of the Christian faith is to Christian experience. Loving Christ is its own justification, as every loving heart knows. Life evidences itself: the existence of light is its own proof. The power of Christ on the heart needs no other argument than itself. Men only doubt when the life has died out, and the light has waned, and flickered, and spent itself. It is when there is no sign of the spirit in our midst, no token of forces beyond the normal and the usual, that we can deny the spirit. It is when faith is not in evidence that we can dispute faith. It is when love is dead that we can question love. The Christian faith is not a creed, but a life; not a proposition, but a passion. Love is its own witness to the soul that loves: communion is its own attestation to the spirit that lives in the fellowship. The man who lives with Jesus knows Him to be a Lover that cleaves closer than a brother, a Friend, that loveth at all times, and a Brother born for adversity.

It does not follow that there is an end of the question, so far as we are concerned, if we say that we at least do not know that friendship, and cannot love Him. Some even say it with a wistful longing, "Oh, that I knew where I might find Him." It is true that love cannot be forced, that it cannot be made to order, that we cannot love because we ought, or even because we want. But we can bring ourselves into the presence of the lovable. We can enter into Friendship through the door of Discipleship; we can learn love through service; and the day will come to us also when the Master's word will be true, "I call you no longer servant, but I call you friend." His love will take possession of us, till all else seems as hatred in comparison. "All lovers blush when ye stand beside Christ," says Samuel Rutherford; "woe unto all love but the love of Christ. Shame forevermore be upon all glory but the glory of Christ; hunger forevermore be upon all heaven but Christ. I cry death, death be upon all manner of life but the life of Christ."

---

* Hugh Black. Friendship, Copyright, 1898, by Fleming H. Revell Company. Reprinted by permission of the publisher. Pp. 219-237.

THE HIGHER FRIENDSHIP * (continued)

To be called friends by our Master, to know Him as the **Lover of** our souls, to give Him entrance to our hearts, is to learn the **meaning** of living, and to experience the ecstasy of living. The **Higher Friend-** ship is bestowed without money and without price, and is **open to** every heart responsive to God's great love.

 " 'Tis only heaven that is given away,
 'Tis God alone may be had for the asking.''

---

* Hugh Black. Friendship, Copyright, 1898, by Fleming H. Revell Company. Reprinted by permission of the publisher. Pp. 219-237.

THE FATHER IS VERY FOND OF ME*

There is yet another way to pray our work and this is to pray in terms of one another. A few years ago I was suggesting small fraternal groups of five or six people but they were not that easy to gather. Today I would speak in terms of two or three, even one other person, a pusher, one to whom I am accountable. Our Lord never sent anyone out alone. He always sent them in two's, two by two. We need to rediscover the law of the gospel and share our prayer with someone. In order to grow in prayer, one needs another person, someone to be brother or sister, something like a center for discernment, decision, fidelity. We have no lack of good will. Our greatest weakness is forgetfulness. We have to make our prayer more visible, our life more transparent. We need someone to help us to be faithful, to be obedient to our own inner grace. We are continually receiving a deep inner grace far beyond what a community can give us and we must be faithful to this grace. We so easily forget; it is so easily lost in the shuffle. We need someone to bring us to this. p. 117

We have to keep the law of the Sabbath. He asks of us the tithing of our time. He does not need our time; we do; otherwise, we will not be free. To ignore the Sabbath is to render ourselves enslaved. "He who works without prayer is a slave." (Mother Teresa). We need to review and to anticipate our lives, what has been and what is to be. We need someone with whom we can celebrate our inner lives. Where two or three are gathered together in his name, something special takes place. p. 118

The root word for "obedience" is the same as it is for the word "pray"; it means to listen. Christ prayed deeply, he listened deeply to the reality of the Father. Jesus revealed not himself, but the Father. He is all that the Father is, and what he is, he has called us to become. Jesus has radicalized our prayer because prayer is not a burden to be done, but the task of becoming not only who we are but who we are all together. The consequence of Christ's prayer was "all that I have learned from the Father, I have made known to you. Because of this, you are my friend."

The root of friendship is prayer, because the root of prayer is presence—presence to all that is. It is not easy to be present to oneself. We spend most of our time in a flight from prayer, which is a flight from ourselves. We can take only so much of ourselves; but

* Edward J. Farrell, The Father Is Very Fond of Me. Copyright (c) 1975 by Edward J. Farrell. Reprinted by permission of Dimension Books, Inc., Denville, N.J. 07834.

THE FATHER IS VERY FOND OF ME * (continued)

it is only in a radical presence to ourselves, in a coming to say "I am," that we can be present to him who is all that we are. Our presence to him becomes a compelling force to be present to others. We can know that we are living in him, that he is living in us because he lets us share his spirit. Open your hearts to one another as he has opened his heart to you, and God will be glorified. Each one of us has been entrusted with a gift which is intended for one another. p. 82

---

* Edward J. Farrell, The Father Is Very Fond of Me. Copyright (c) 1975 by Edward J. Farrell. Reprinted by permission of Dimension Books, Inc., Denville, N.J. 07834.

No. 2 — BECOMING A FAITHFUL FRIEND

N.B.   Read carefully all instructions on this page before beginning to fulfill them.

A.   Think about:

— What a faithful friend is (See following page)

B.   Begin to practice: (See pages in this section, No. 2, following)

— Disciplines

— Meditation — the Gateway to Prayer

— The Practice of the Principles of Faithful Friendship

— The Keeping of a Journal (2 pages)

C.   Read carefully — and "ponder these things in your heart":

— A Close Look at Faithful Friendship

— On Being Present Where You Are

— The Link with the Center

— Ring of Yourself

D.   Pray daily for yourself and for your 'faithful friend' —

using Psalm 23 which is a beautiful example of meditation leading into prayer.

"The Lord is my shepherd . . ."

"The Lord is Jane's shepherd, she shall not want . . ."
(name of faithful friend)

E.   Prepare a short accountability report for your faithful friend (see paragraph on accountability report on page entitled "A Close Look at Faithful Friendship").

WHAT A FAITHFUL FRIEND IS

A faithful friend is a sure shelter,
   whoever finds one has found a rare treasure.
A faithful friend is something beyond price,
   there is no measuring his worth.
A faithful friend is the elixir of life,
   and those who fear the Lord will find one.
Whoever fears the Lord makes true friends,
   for as a man is, so is his friend.   (Ecclesiasticus 6: 14-17 Jer.)

"Friend" — from the Anglo Saxon word "freond" — originally the
   present participle of the verb meaning to love
"Faithful" — means full of faith (trust) in God.
   One whose "ultimate concern" is God.

   Therefore, a faithful friend is a loving one full of faith in God.

   To be faithful is to have God's greatest gift—the Spirit of
      Christ—abiding in one.

      "Abide in me, and I in you." (John 15)
      "That we may be one." (John 17)

   To be faithful also means to be 'doing the works of God'—
      believing "in Him whom He has sent"   (John 6:28 RSV)
      for, if "you do not have his word abiding in you . . . you do
      not believe him whom he has sent."   (John 6:38 RSV)

A friend is someone who leaves you with all your freedom intact,
   but who obliges you to be fully what you are.

Oh
   the comfort, the inexpressible comfort of feeling safe with a person,
   having neither to weigh thoughts nor measure words,
      but pouring them all right out, just as they are —
         chaff and grain together —
   certain that a faithful hand will take and sift them,
      keep what is worth keeping,
         and with the breath of kindness blow the rest away.*

A friend may well be reckoned the masterpiece of nature. (Emerson)

* "Friendship" by Dinah Maria Mulock Craik, from The Best Loved Poems of the American People selected by Hazel Felleman. Copyright 1936, Doubleday & Company, Inc., 245 Park Avenue, New York, N.Y. 10017, p. 43.

DISCIPLINES

— Endeavor to grow in the practice of the principles of faithful friendship. The principles cover both the inward and the outward journey, having to do with one's relationship with God, with one's admitted "faithful friend", and with every other human relationship whether it be casual or constant.

— A daily time apart:

for meditation on Scripture with emphasis on the Gospels for we believe it to be urgent to steep our minds and hearts in Christ, The Faithful Friend of all.

for prayer including prayer for the faithful friend, with emphasis on listening in the silence.

— Journal keeping — recording spiritual insights, moods of joy and depression, dreams, reactions to events, persons, or reading matter—anything that has been particularly meaningful.

— Accountability — Weekly exchange with faithful friend of written account concerning disciplines kept or neglected; what the Scripture has revealed to me; crucial problems or peak experiences of my life during the week—this account to be returned for inclusion in journal.

— Collateral reading — to be selected with care.

— Tithing (as a minimum) with careful and continuing consideration of our use of money as the sure indication of "where one's heart is."

— Corporate Worship — weekly.

MEDITATION — The Gateway to Prayer

PREPARATION — Determine the subject of your meditation before your time for meditation. If your time is in the morning (and that is usually the best time)— it is helpful to read over the material the night before.

NOTEBOOK — Provide yourself with a loose-leaf notebook. Use it as a journal—and for "jottings" of insights, prayers, things you may want to recall.

TIME — Set aside a time, every day, preferably the same time—not less than ten minutes, which you devote to meditation. (See paper entitled "The Link with the Center.")

PLACE — Find a place where you will be least likely to be disturbed—as quiet a place as possible— preferably the same place daily —

> And so I find it well to come
> For deeper rest to this still room,
> For here the habit of the soul
> Feels less the outer world's control;
> And from the silence multiplied
> By these still forms on either side,
> The world that time and sense has known
> Falls off and leaves us God alone.

ATTITUDE — Be expectant.
"Behold, I stand at the door and knock;
if any one hears my voice and opens
the door,
I will come in to him . . ." (Rev. 3:30 RSV).

METHOD — If you find that you need the spur and help of a method of meditation, inquire about methods; choose one, read about it, and put it into practice. Do not use it slavishly. Use it only until you develop your own way. The whole point of a method is to help you to meditate— and so to pray.

As a beginning, St. Francis de Sales offers two suggestions: As you "settle in" for your quiet time —

1. Remember that you are in the presence of God.

2. Ask God to inspire your time.

THE PRACTICE OF THE PRINCIPLES OF FAITHFUL FRIENDSHIP

<u>Autobiography</u>—to be given to your faithful friend at the beginning of your relationship. Recalling and recording what to you seem to have been the formative influences in, and effects upon your life—the forces, circumstances, persons, and events that have made you the person you are—will be enlightening not only to your friend but to you as well. One or both of you may even discern a pattern or a sequence in your life that you never before knew was there.

<u>Presence</u> — Practice being truly "present" to your faithful friend.

Listen — to him/her during personal contacts
— for him/her during personal prayer time

To "listen another's soul into a condition of disclosure and discovery may be almost the greatest service that any human being ever performs for another." *

<u>Communication with faithful friend</u> — to be frequent.

Place of Meeting — Preferably the same place each time—a quiet place—free, if possible from disturbance and interruption.

Time of Meeting — Reserving the same time each week on your calendar for meeting with your friend affords necessary continuity and rhythm, and precludes conflicts in your schedule. (Telephone calls are no substitute.)

Your first meeting could perhaps be limited to one hour, but as you endeavor to embrace the disciplines and practices of faithful friendship you will need and want at least a two-hour period.

---

* Douglas V. Steere, <u>On Beginning from Within/On Listening to Another,</u> Copyright (c) 1943, 1955, 1964 by Douglas V. Steere. Reprinted by permission of Harper & Row, Publishers, Inc. (p. 198).

THE PRACTICE OF THE PRINCIPLES OF FAITHFUL FRIENDSHIP
(continued)

Suggested Structure of Meeting-time—

Begin with at least a minute or two of silence in which to become "collected"—to remind yourselves silently that you are together in the presence of your mutual Faithful Friend who, if you defer to him and listen to him, will guide and inspire your time. As your relationship with him and with your faithful friend deepens, your time of shared silence will lengthen and grow more meaning-filled and more precious.

Meditate on the Scriptures suggested in the materials you have studied and pondered during the current week—and "think aloud" with one another about them.

Listen to each other with your inner ear—as you communicate to one another how your reading and daily meditation and praying have changed or affected your everyday life—or perhaps have not. If they have—consider that. If they have not, why not?

Service — Be available to your faithful friend in every possible way.

  Seek to be helpful in concrete ways—to be understanding —to be sympathetic.

  Never shirk or side-step confrontation when confrontation is necessary, but always proceed with discretion and with love.

Verbal Witness — Speak the truth in love as you are enabled to speak it from your own experience—humbly and honestly.

Suggestions concerning THE KEEPING of a JOURNAL

1. Obtain a good loose-leaf notebook to use for your journal. Loose-leaf notebook pages (standard 8½″ x 5½″) will fit within the pages of this handbook.

2. Date every entry with day, month, and year.

3. Write whatever you want to write—what is on your mind, such as:
   — significant happenings, decisions, insights;
   — a description of your mood of the moment;
   — an appraisal of your day (or of the day before);
   — hopes, fears, concerns, joys;
   — assessment of a relationship with your own inner (true) self, with another person, with God, with material things, with events;
   — a "peak experience," or a failure or success in trying to fulfill what you believe is God's will for you to be or to do.

   This is your journal, for your eyes only unless you sometime consider it helpful (for the sake of another or for your own sake) to share a part of it with someone whose discretion and discernment you trust.

4. Record your insights from times of meditation and prayer, revelation or enlightenment.

5. Record every dream you have when you can remember it, or any part of it.

   a. In the hazy, half-waking time when you begin to be aware of having dreamed, train yourself to remain perfectly still and try to remember the dream in its entirety. Even the slightest move can sometimes make the memory of the dream vanish. Having remembered the dream, if it is an involved one, jot down single words or phrases to remind you of its content before you start to write it out. This procedure is especially helpful if you have dreamed two or three separate dreams— or more. Record the whole dream or dreams immediately if this is possible. Keep your journal close at hand.

   b. Include all the details, insignificant as they may seem.

   c. Think about the dream trying to determine what your inner self may be trying to convey to you—or what your inner self has been trying to work through while you slept—while your active attention to other things was at rest.

   d. Drawing a sketch of the setting or the scene of your dream may prove helpful. You don't have to be artistic—just draw as best you can—using stick figures—anything that helps to clarify the scene or the action of the dream.

   e. It is better to record your dreams as a part of your chronological journal rather than in a separate section of your notebook because of their probable relevance to your current activities. You may find that your dreams reflect your spiritual progress or retrogression.

THE KEEPING of a JOURNAL (continued)

6. It is often helpful to write out a prayer—almost like a letter to your Heavenly Father—pouring out your feelings just as they are, tumbling over one another seeking expression, or slowly wrung from out the depths of you. It is good to do this at varying times when you may be keenly aware of:
   - frustrating distractions
   - immense gratitude for grace received
   - discouragement bordering on despair
   - need for confession
   - overwhelming desire to fulfill God's will in your life— willing fervently to will His will.

7. As your journal grows, you may find it helpful to have an index with references according to date so that you can find them easily. Such an index might include:
   - names of persons (included in your journal notes, dreams, or prayers)
   - insights, experiences, topics to which you might want to be able to turn readily.

8. You might profit by having a separate section of your journal (or even a separate notebook) devoted to a kind of bibliography of books containing helpful passages related to your topical index —or you might even have the excerpts themselves included in your notebook.

SOME PRIMARY USES OF THE JOURNAL

1. Writing in your journal is one way to articulate and thus to clarify in your own mind your moods, feelings, motives, hopes, fears, loves, hates, ambitions, sufferings, joys,—all facets of your life. Such clarification makes it possible to determine your ultimate goal and the directions in which you move toward or away from that goal.

2. What matters most is your direction—not how far along you are. There is no point in comparing yourself with others—but there is validity in comparing yourself as you are today with yourself as you were a month ago, a year ago, five years ago. You can answer such questions as:
   - Are you wrestling with the same old problems?
   - Is your direction the same?
   - What about your patience? Is it increasing?—decreasing?
   - Are you understanding any more clearly what it must mean to pray without ceasing?

3. Your journal is a storehouse of your own written prayers. When you are "down" it is good to read one of your prayers recorded when you were "up"—to help you remember that the spiritual journey is a succession of valleys, plateaus, peaks—not a sojourn in any one spot.

A CLOSE LOOK AT FAITHFUL FRIENDSHIP

The primary principle of faithful friendship is the conscious endeavor to accept the proffered friendship of Jesus Christ and to develop a heightened awareness of the significance of having Jesus Christ as Faithful Friend.

Having this primary relationship enables one to be a faithful friend and:

> Offers opportunity to learn to listen:
> — to listen in prayer—to the Father of both you and your friend. (Intercession for another can be offering yourself in prayer to the Father to be used as He directs.)
>
> — to listen, really listen, to your friend
> Genuine listening can enable you to 'hear' not only what your friend wants to articulate but also what he may not say but which, nonetheless, needs to be heard. There are few persons who know how to listen.
>
> > — Most persons are too eager to speak to be able to listen.
> > — Self-interest is so great that it defeats interest in others. (There is no one from whom we cannot learn something.)

Offers opportunity on a one-to-one basis to share the things that matter to Christians endeavoring to grow in the life of the spirit. Realization that the Spirit of Christ is always present as the third in your small group of two will make your written and personal sharing fruitful.

> Accountability to one another:
> > — will shed light on strengths and weaknesses in maintaining disciplines having to do with Scripture, meditation, prayer, relationships, money, and individual and corporate worship.
> > — will foster confession.
> > — will give rise to healthy confrontation without incurring alienation.
> > — will prevent compartmentalizing "spiritual" and "secular" lives as each week disclosure is made of crucial problems and peak experiences.

A CLOSE LOOK AT FAITHFUL FRIENDSHIP (continued)

Develops within, and between friends:

Humility — It requires greater humility to open your heart to a friend than it would to open your heart to an acknowledged spiritual director like Gordon Cosby, Douglas Steere, John Coburn, Dom John Chapman, Thomas Merton, St. John of the Cross (if any of them were available).

Trust — that the one to whom you are speaking from the heart will honor your confidence in him as you honor his confidence in you.

Knowledge — true knowledge of one another. In biblical language, knowledge is not merely the conclusion of an intellectual process but the fruit of an experience, a personal contact; when it matures, it is love.

Love — which is the whole commandment that includes all others.

Unity — "that we may all be one"—that quality of at-oneness in Christ—"joined and knit together by every joint . . . each part working properly" for the fulfillment of mission.

ON BEING PRESENT WHERE YOU ARE

A real friend is present. He is there when you need him. A real friend seems to know the word to speak, or the question to ask, or the book to send in order to help to restore for us the lost image of our life task. He knows how to confirm in us the deepest thing that is already there, "answering to that of God" in his needy friend. p. 16

Presence may also come in an act of prayer. For in the life of prayer we bring ourselves into an openness that makes it possible for us to be freshly aware of God's presence. It is not that he is not present at other times but that by this voluntary act of ours, the act of prayer, we are enabled to break with our outer preoccupations and to become aware of the presence and of what that presence does to search and to transform and to renew us and to send us back into life again.

A speaker was once introduced by the perfect chairman who said simply, "Mr. Weaver, we are ready. Are you ready?" When I gather myself for prayer it is almost as if God were so addressing me: "Douglas Steere, I am ready. Are you ready?" And my answer is, "O

---

* From On Being Present Where You Are by Douglas V. Steere, Pendle Hill Pamphlet 151, (c) 1967 by Pendle Hill, Wallingford, Pa. 19086.

ON BEING PRESENT WHERE YOU ARE,* continued

Lord, you are always ready but am I ever ready? O Lord, make me ready, or at least make me more ready to be made ready." pp. 17-18

In intercessory prayer, however, where I and my friend may be acutely present to each other and to the ground of infinite compassionate love, it is not only my friend who is irradiated and opened to transformation but this holds for my own life as well, for two persons can never be truly present to each other or to the living God and remain the same. When E. Herman says, "To come near to God is to change," she might as readily have said, "To be present to God, either alone or in the presence of another, is to change," for to be present is to be open to influence. pp. 18-19

In all areas: personal, ecumenical, educational, racial, political— to be present, really present, is to be vulnerable, to be able to be hurt. And when pain is in prospect, it is so much easier to be elsewhere than where we are. p. 34

How much interior emigration there is all about us! Students emigrate to the future and are not present where they are. Displaced persons live in the past and refuse to let go to the new homeland and to live where they are. Parents are not present here and now but are living for the day when the children are raised, or when they will retire, or when they will be free of this or that, but remain numb and glazed and absent from the living moment. To be present is to be vulnerable, to be able to be hurt, to be willing to be spent—but it is also to be awake, alive, and engaged actively in the immediate assignment that has been laid upon us. p. 35

There is One who, on that road out of Jerusalem to the little town of Emmaus, taught his companions of the road and of the table what it was to be present. "Did not our hearts burn within us while he talked with us by the way?" That same quickening presence still walks by our side. That same presence kindles our meetings for worship and reveals to us our failure to be truly present with our families, our friends, and our brothers in the world. It is there in his presence when we are again given the gift of tears, that we are once more joined to all the living, that hope is restored in us, and that we are rebaptized into the sacredness of the gift of life and of the gift of being set down here among fellow humans who, in the depth of their being, long to be truly present to each other. Not only is there "no time but this present," but there is no task God has called us to, as Friends, that is more exciting and challenging than being made inwardly ready to be present where we are. p. 36

* From On Being Present Where You Are by Douglas V. Steere, Pendle Hill Pamphlet 151, (c) 1967 by Pendle Hill, Wallingford, Pa. 19086.

THE LINK WITH THE CENTER

Modern man is in danger of losing his innermost centre which gives stability to his personality and direction to his way of life. Behind the facade of talk and ceaseless activities he becomes unsure of himself; beneath his self-assured persona there is an ever-increasing anxiety. To counteract this trend he must rediscover the point of inner support from which he can issue forth into the world and to which he can return again and again.* (pp. 11-12).

Collectedness . . . means that man becomes composed and concentrated. Usually he is distracted by the diversity of objects and events; agitated by friendly or hostile contacts; assailed by desires, fear, care or passion. He is constantly bent on achieving something, or on warding off something; on acquiring or rejecting; on building up or destroying. Man always wants something, and to want means to be on the way, either towards a goal or away from a danger. This has been so ever since man existed and is even more so with modern man. Man likes to think of himself as active, striving and creative. In this he is only partly right. He would in fact be even more right if he thought of himself as a restless being, incapable of standing still or of concentrating; as one who uses up people, things, thoughts and words without, however, finding fulfilment; as a being who has lost the link with the centre and who, with all his knowledge and abilities, is a victim of chance. This restless being wants to pray—can he do it? Only if he steps out of the stream of restlessness and composes himself.* (p. 16).

This means discarding roaming desires and concentrating on that thing alone which, for the time being, is the only one that matters. He must detach himself and say: 'Now there is nothing which concerns me, except prayer. The next ten minutes'—or whatever time he may have allocated to it—'are reserved for this. Everything else is excluded, I am completely free and dedicated to this one task,' and he must be completely honest in this, for man is an artful creature and the artfulness of his heart asserts itself in religious matters. No sooner has he started to pray than, conjured up by his inner unrest, all sorts of things clamour for attention. All matter of things: a job of work, a conversation, an errand, a newspaper, a book. All these suddenly appear most important, and prayer seems a sheer waste of time. But no sooner has he stopped praying than there is plenty of time, and he fritters it away with useless activities. To collect oneself means to overcome this deception which springs from unrest and to become still; to free oneself of everything which is irrelevant, and to hold oneself at the disposal of God, who alone matters now.* (pp. 16-17).

---

* From Prayer in Practice by Romano Guardini, translated by Prince Leopold of Loewenstein-Wertheim. Copyright 1957 by Pantheon Books, a Division of Random House, Inc. Reprinted by permission of the publisher.

THE LINK WITH THE CENTER (continued)

We may express this differently by saying that what matters is that man should become present. This unrest which grips us when we are about to pray may also be defined as an urge.to be somewhere else. We can yield to this urge by getting up and going, either into the next room or into the street or to the office; or we may look out of the window or take up a book or think of something else . . . Always this inner unrest drives us away from the place where we should be, i.e., the here and the duty. This is the place where things really matter, where one must hold one's ground; the place where the Living God calls to the self—the place of obedience. In this exacting stillness man begins to feel uncomfortable and tries to run away . . . It would appear that man, the more firmly he is rooted in the world, the more adrift he becomes from the place which really matters.* (p. 17).

If he wants to pray, he must recall himself from everything and everywhere and become and remain present. This 'remaining' is difficult, for only on rare occasions do we meet with an experience so definite and compelling as to hold us and make us willing to remain for a while. Yet everything depends on this ability to stand still and to be present with full inner awareness.* (p. 17).

There is an outer RING OF YOURSELF ** surrounded by turbulence, chaos and anxiety; great moments swirling about, cosmic in potentiality.[1] Within this ring is another circle outside of which are your responses to all these alarms and insistent shocks, excitements and dismays.[2] Inside this ring is another ring. This is a place where you sense your ignorances, your unawarenesses, your inadequacies. Here is where you are sorely tried, for this is your human self.[3] And so these rings get smaller as you near the center where you find a place in you that longs for peace, calmness and spiritual understanding.[4] Finally there is the center which seems to the imagination within a very small circumference. Here is where you are, here is a place where you decide; here is where you are yourself. Most people seldom find it except in great moments; and yet when found and realized it encircles the universe. This is the quietness, this is the peace promised to those who seek. For this center lifts you high and clear of all the rings into eternal omniscient vision. Here, when your mind is fastened

---

* From Prayer in Practice by Romano Guardini, translated by Prince Leopold of Loewenstein-Wertheim. Copyright 1957 by Pantheon Books, a Division of Random House, Inc. Reprinted by permission of the publisher.

** From Letters of the Scattered Brotherhood edited by Mary Strong. Copyright 1948 by Harper & Row, Publishers, Inc. Reprinted by permission of publisher.

RING OF YOURSELF * (continued)

to it and all your thoughts and all desires are pointed toward it, is the Spirit that will lead you through the valleys of the shadows of death, violence and hates and all the confusion that beset you and your country and your world at this time.[5] (pp. 180-181).

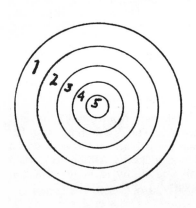

Hold to this center. You can only reach it in silence, you can only keep it in quietness, you can only feel it in serenity; this is the place of the pearl of great price. Carry the silence of your guarded center with you, guarded by the thoughts you have accepted. This is the way of a son of God. Every man in ordinary life presents a character which is instantly felt; everyone is revealed sooner or later, the vagaries of the human personality betray us. But the quietness of the realm I speak of is a steadying strength not of our making though of our accepting, and what is given forth from it is felt also. (p. 181).

Remember always to acknowledge this: "of myself I can do nothing." What you have done is to seek the kingdom and having found it your task is to hold it, and that is a task indeed, for emotions, personalities can steal you away out among the outer rings; your thoughts, instead of being pointed toward your center, race away into the mad dance. (p. 181).

Come back, come back and in holy stillness be lifted high above all this! Your dominion over yourself and the circumstances of your life can be glorious if you will keep your center clean, illumined and still in immortal silence. Here is selflessness, here is revealed true knowledge, wisdom, power and courage; the dignity of courage which is loyal to that which is not your human self. You will be given divine strategy in dealing with seemingly hopeless difficulties. The hates, criticisms, annoyances, the instinctive dislikes . . . keep them in the outer circumference. Turn your face away, turn it within toward that which is shining there. This is the kingdom of heaven. This is the task most needed now for yourself, for your loved ones, for your time. Each one anchored in this omnipotent stillness strengthens the soul of your nation. "I never leave thee nor forsake thee, thou art in my keeping." (pp. 181-182).

---

* From Letters of the Scattered Brotherhood edited by Mary Strong. Copyright 1948 by Harper & Row, Publishers, Inc. Reprinted by permission of publisher.

"You shall love your
neighbor as yourself."
(Matt. 22:39 RSV)

No. 3 — I MUST LOVE MYSELF

N.B. Always read carefully at the beginning of the week all instructions on page outlining structure for the week.

A. MEDITATE and PRAY daily, using pages on "Vocal Prayer—Mental Prayer—Meditation" each day of the week, beginning tomorrow.

Do not neglect to pray for your "faithful friend."

B. STUDY the Menninger paper and

WRITE OUT (for yourself) the answers to the seven questions.

C. PREPARE ACCOUNTABILITY REPORT to give to your faithful friend.

D. MAKE DAILY ENTRY in your journal—no matter how brief. This will help to develop the habit.

VOCAL PRAYER — MENTAL PRAYER — MEDITATION

1st day

Vocal prayer: Prayer in words, made aloud or silently, repeated from memory, or read, or composed by oneself.

Mental prayer: Prayer, aloud or silent, made thoughtfully and with understanding of what is being said, to Whom it is being said, and "who we are who address the Lord."

Meditation: Thinking and pondering—in the Presence of God —upon the specific meaning for us, personally, of some words we have read or some thought we have had.

". . . the most promising method of prayer is to allow oneself to be guided by the (Word), to pray on the basis of a word of Scripture. In this way we shall not become the victims of our own emptiness.* (p. 84).

". . . let those of you who cannot meditate . . . or keep your thoughts fixed on God without being greatly distracted, try earnestly to acquire this habit: Imagine our Lord beside you and see how lovingly and humbly He teaches you.** (p. 155).

"Often we are so burdened and overwhelmed with other thoughts, images, and concerns that it may take a long time before God's Word has swept all else aside and come through. But it will surely come, just as surely as God Himself has come to men and will come again. This is the very reason why we begin our meditation with the prayer that God may send His Holy Spirit to us through His Word and reveal His Word to us and enlighten us.* (pp. 82-83).

MEDITATE on Ephesians 3: 14-21—then pray this prayer of Paul's for yourself, changing pronouns from "you" to "me," "your" to "my," etc.

2nd day

"It is not necessary that we should discover new ideas in our meditation. Often this only diverts us and feeds our vanity. It is sufficient if the Word, as we read and understand it, penetrates and dwells within us . . . in meditation God's Word seeks to enter in and remain with us. It strives to stir us, to work and operate in us, so that we shall not get away from it the whole day long. Then it will do its work in us, often without our being conscious of it. * (p. 83).

MEDITATE: on John 3:16; John 7:37-38; John 8:12   PRAY

---

* Dietrich Bonhoeffer, Life Together, Copyright 1954 by Harper & Row, Publishers, Inc. Reprinted by permission of the publisher.

** St. Theresa, Way of Perfection, Copyright 1946, The Newman Bookshop. Reprinted by permission of Paulist Press.

VOCAL PRAYER — MENTAL PRAYER — MEDITATION (continued)

3rd day

"Above all, it is not necessary that we should have any unexpected, extraordinary experiences in meditation. This can happen, but if it does not, it is not a sign that the meditation period has been useless. Not only at the beginning, but repeatedly, there will be times when we feel a great spiritual dryness and apathy, an aversion, even an inability to meditate. We dare not be balked by such experiences. Above all, we must not allow them to keep us from adhering to our meditation period with great patience and fidelity . . . 'Seek God, not happiness'—this is the fundamental rule of all meditation. If you seek God alone, you will gain happiness; that is its promise.* (pp. 83-84)

MEDITATE on Matthew 6:25-33; Matthew 7:7-14.   PRAY

4th day

"When they pray, men have to begin where they are. If they are obsessed and clogged up with loneliness and self-pity and a feeling of injustice, how can they be sincere if they do not pour out these sentiments? Veterans of prayer are not shocked at these things. They only insist that the person persevere, continue in the prayer, pray it through until the foreground becomes aware of the background. For in prayer, real prayer, what a man brings is irradiated by a power that loosens the arms that are carrying all these bundles of defective goods, bent on returning them to the merchant with bitter abuse, and the arms relax, and the bundles fall away, and the errand seems unimportant, in fact ridiculously unimportant and the question arises. 'What is God willing to have me learn from this time of aloneness? What new step of yielding is He asking of me now? What can I do for Him in my situation?' And the person stops talking and begins to listen. What does it matter how self-involved a prayer or a conversation begins if it beats its way through to such an awareness? For in this tendered openness, the membrane between the soul of man and the living Listener is almost as if it did not exist at all.** (p. 212)

MEDITATE on Matthew 11:25-30   PRAY

---

* Dietrich Bonhoeffer, Life Together, Copyright 1954 by Harper & Row, Publishers, Inc. Reprinted by permission of the publisher.

** Douglas V. Steere, On Beginning from Within/On Listening to Another. Copyright (c) 1943, 1955, 1964 by Douglas V. Steere. Reprinted by permission of Harper & Row, Publishers, Inc.

VOCAL PRAYER — MENTAL PRAYER — MEDITATION (continued)

5th day

"Who can compel love? We often ask; and how can we, whose spirits blow where they list, obey a command to love the Unseen? In meditation we may find an answer. We love God so little because we know Him so imperfectly. Who loves a chance acquaintance? The unknown may, and does exert an initial attraction; but our response depends upon our knowledge. In valid meditation that knowledge dawns and grows. Thoughts come to us which are no mere intellectual apprehensions, but lay compelling hands upon emotion and will. Through them the love of God is shed abroad in our hearts, and ere we know it we respond in some measure. We must needs love, since He has first loved us. . . . To be made in God's image is to be made to love Him. . . . The meditation which does not waken love in our hearts, however poor and feeble that beginning of love may be, is imperfect; for where God and the soul really meet, there the intelligence, the will and the emotions rise together, and what before was hearsay of conventional theology becomes self-evident truth. God reveals Himself as the supreme loving and lovable One; and love is continually communicating, propagating and begetting itself.*
(p. 83-84). MEDITATE on John 14:1-15.   PRAY

6th day

"The difference between the saints of old and ourselves is not one of inherent nature; it is simply that they took time to ponder God, to gaze upon Him in an act of supreme attention in which intelligent will and desire concurred in perfect harmony, while we are too greatly overrun with small activities and occupations to find leisure for such pondering. No human being . . . who has really set himself to live in the thought of God but has felt the glow of a new affection, the unsealing of a fountain of love within. (Psalm 1:1-3).

And as we ponder and are silent, that Love will utter its unspoken demands. In some form or other, we shall hear the cry, 'My son, give Me thy heart.' And on our answer to that cry hangs our destiny.*
(p. 85). MEDITATE on Matthew 16:24-26.   PRAY

7th day

Review your jottings for the week . . . and meditate again on that passage which was most meaningful to you.   PRAY

---

* E. Herman, Creative Prayer. Harper & Row. 1940. Reprinted by permission of Harper & Row, Publishers, Inc.

RESPONSIBILITY to SELF *

In this incredibly complex world, each of us needs to examine ourselves—our motivations, our goals. As a search for a clearer idea of what we stand for, toward what we are headed and what we think is truly important, this kind of continuing self-scrutiny can help to stabilize us in a world of explosive change. A close look at ourselves contributes to that sought-after capacity for autonomy, and gives us greater ability to make wise and useful choices, to exert some control over our own destiny.

It is never easy for any of us to look closely at ourselves—the ancient aphorism of "physician, heal thyself" notwithstanding. Most of us do so only when forced by crisis, anxiety, or a blunt confrontation with reality. Some of us have spouses or friends who help us look at the sore spots within, the personal rough spots which cause us and others pain. But, for most of us, it is far easier to look outside, to look at others, whether to admire or to find fault, whether to seek guidance or to castigate.

As important as this self-knowledge is, the daily pressures to act, to do, to decide make it difficult to stop and think, to consider, to examine one's life goals, one's directions, one's priorities—the basic choices one faces in managing his own world. Indeed, it is more than probable that few of us would pause to undertake such a vital inventory unless someone else said, as I am saying now, "Stop! Think about these issues for a while; defer those other 'important' things that preempt your daily routine!"

How are we to go about this? I ask you to focus on several rhetorical questions—rhetorical because the answers are to be offered to yourself, not to the public scene. The questions are intended to be a framework around which you may organize ideas about yourself and your relationships with your environment. Though they are questions which focus on the inner world, though they are here raised by a psychiatrist, and though they might be considered a kind of "mental health check-up," they will unquestionably strike you as rather non-medical, and perhaps even more philosophic than scientific. But preeminently they are intended to provoke honest thought—never an easy task in relation to one's self.

* Roy Menninger, "Responsibility to Self," Menninger Perspective, June/July 1972. Reprinted by permission of the Menninger Foundation.

RESPONSIBILITY to SELF * (continued)

I. The first of these questions is perhaps the most global, for it
invites a review of your basic life direction: What are your goals
in life? Put otherwise, toward what objectives are you aiming and
how realistic are they? How well do they incorporate what is really
important to you, and how well do they accurately express your
values? Are they for real, or only for show?

The network of queries arising from the central question provokes
several observations. In an era when planning and setting objectives
are bywords for every organization, it is ironic to see how few people
have adopted the same strategy for themselves. Perhaps only in late
middle-age does the lack of a clear sense of direction and the absence of specific goals become an appalling reality. Many people
reach that point in life with a bitter sense of loss and regret, won-
dering where time and opportunity have gone. The lack of intrinsic
value in the materialistically oriented goals some people adopt is
obvious when they helplessly wonder what to do next with their lives,
now that they have the million dollars they planned to make. The
acquisition of a bigger house, a bigger boat, plus all the status that
money will buy has taken on the appearance of a logical goal for
many—but would that truly represent your central values?

One cannot think about one's own life goals without asking still
other difficult questions: To what purpose do you dedicate your
efforts and your lives? What are your personal priorities, and how
well does your life's work reflect those priorities? Most of us find
such difficult questions easy to avoid, presuming that time will
answer them—as indeed it will, though not necessarily to our ultimate satisfaction. A close, comfortable and accepting relationship
with another person—a spouse, a colleague, a friend, or even a
psychotherapist—can be of great help in considering such questions.
The dilemma is, will you find such an opportunity?

II. Closely related to the question about goals is one which bears on
your use of time and energy: Does your use of your vital resources truly reflect your priorities? Without much thought most of
you would certainly answer "yes," failing to appreciate that for 90
per cent of us the answer is almost assuredly "no." Executives with
broad responsibilities are presumed to use their time for the things

---

* Roy Menninger, "Responsibility to Self," Menninger Perspective, June/July
1972. Reprinted by permission of the Menninger Foundation.

RESPONSIBILITY to SELF * (continued)

that are important—such things as planning, policy preparation, and the "big" decisions. With a consistency that is hard to believe, studies have repeatedly shown that this is rarely true, and that much more often the busy executive is spending 90 per cent of his time on matters that could better be done by others, are simply a part of the daily routine and have very limited relation to the vital responsibilities which he carries.

Most of us will recognize in a moment of more somber thought that the "important things" in our lives are frequently deferred with some comforting but self-deceiving assumption that there will always be time tomorrow.

From yet another perspective, there is a high probability that your use of time and energy reflects serious imbalances within the life space of each of you. In spite of such public protestations about the importance of the family, about the needs of the community, about the troubles in our world, most of us devote the smallest proportion of our time to these areas. Indeed, it could be fairly said of many of you that you are married to your jobs, not your husbands or wives, that you are invested in your colleagues, not your children, that you are committed to your business, not your society. The point is not that these imbalances are wrong, but that it is quite probable that they are decidedly inconsistent with your own statements about what is important and what constitute your personal priorities.

It is this inconsistency which produces a subtle but corrosive tension as your conscience cries out for one commitment while your activities express another. At times this reflects a distorted conception of responsibility, at times an impulsive response to the demands of others, but most often it is the outcome of unthinking behavior, the consequence of a general failure to consider your goals, your priorities, and your plans for reaching them.

Nowhere is the imbalance in the use of time and energy more obvious than in regard to ourselves. Executives are dedicated people, and for many this dedication implies and finally comes to mean considerable self-sacrifice. Time for one's self is discouraged, pleasure is deemed to be selfish, and one's own needs come last.

---

* Roy Menninger, "Responsibility to Self," Menninger Perspective, June/July 1972. Reprinted by permission of the Menninger Foundation.

RESPONSIBILITY to SELF * (continued)

Again drawing upon information from a study of executives, I can report that less than 40 per cent of some 4000 executives studied had an avocational pursuit. They appeared to have had few sources of personal gratification and gave themselves few opportunities for fulfilling personal pursuits. Why do they not think better of themselves than that, and are they so different from you?

III. The third question is to ask if your sense of responsibility is also out of balance. In its extreme forms, it is easy to find examples of those who will assume no more responsibility for anything than absolutely necessary; certainly the fragmentation of our contemporary culture encourages us to restrict our efforts to smaller and smaller sectors of the human community. Executives demonstrate that same pattern, pointing out that the quantity of information is so great that fragmented specialization' is inevitable and even advisable. And perhaps it is, but are we guilty of hiding an unduly narrow concept of our responsibility to others behind that rationalization?

Considerably more common in the field of industry is a pattern that reflects the other extreme: an excessive sense of responsibility that keeps us moving like a driven animal. Again, the needs of our organization and the endless call for our services make it hard to define a sense of responsibility which simultaneously expresses our commitment to our organization, to ourselves, and to our family and world as well. Failing to do so exposes us to the ravages of guilty feelings of failure, and of all the feelings known to the human psyche, guilt is probably the most painful.

It is easy to confuse a concept of responsibility with a command for action, connecting a notion of obligation with a need to do something about it. When one begins to discover how big the problem is about which he is worrying, his growing sense of helplessness leads him to turn away, disconnect, and assume that someone else will worry instead.

A more difficult but more effective concept of responsibility is an acknowledgment of the importance of continuing to think about problems and dilemmas, neither turning away in frustration nor hurling one's self forward into them under the pressure of guilt. Continuing to think about the problems of delinquency in one's community, the need for better school programs for the limited as well as the gifted, and the hundreds of other things for which responsible concern is needed is a way of staying engaged, remaining open to alternatives

---

* Roy Menninger, "Responsibility to Self," Menninger Perspective, June/July 1972. Reprinted by permission of the Menninger Foundation.

RESPONSIBILITY to SELF * (continued)

and opportunities and being ready to respond when the occasion permits.

In more personal terms, the concept of balanced responsibility implies a willingness to accept the responsibility for one's own attitudes, feelings, failures, and prejudices, forsaking the easier and unfortunately more frequent tendency to project or displace these feelings and attitudes onto persons or forces external to one's self. It is worth asking: Does each of you demonstrate a readiness to acknowledge your anger, your bias, or your limitations—at least to yourself, and to others when this is germane to the situation?

IV. My fourth query is to ask about your courage—not the sort more commonly associated with the battlefield, challenging or embarrassing situations or the like—important though that is. I refer to the courage we need to face the internal foe, for we are in most cases our own worst enemies. In the inimitable words of Pogo, "We have met the enemy—and they is us." This kind of courage is exemplified in an ability to look at yourself honestly and fairly—an expression of the responsibility I noted earlier. It is not easy to entertain the questions I am posing without fluctuating wildly between extremes of excessive personal criticism and total denial that these thoughts have any bearing on you at all.

It is this courage which enables us to face, to articulate and finally to accept our disappointments and losses—one of the most difficult tasks the human psyche faces.

Perhaps this is not so apparent until one stops to realize that life itself is a succession of losses—beginning with the loss of the warmth and comfort of the uterus which nurtured us for the first nine months of our existence; progressing through childhood and its many losses: dependent infant status, our favorite childhood toys, our privileged status; the loss of the family as adolescence separates us from childhood; the loss of the irresponsible pleasures of youth with the advent of maturity; the loss of jobs, or positions, or self-esteem, money, opportunity; the loss of one's friends with advancing age; these and a million others, and finally the ultimate loss of life itself. It is something to ponder how extensive the experience of each of us is with loss, big and small, and to note that these are experiences with profound effects upon our mental health. Even as

---

* Roy Menninger, "Responsibility to Self," Menninger Perspective, June/July 1972. Reprinted by permission of the Menninger Foundation.

RESPONSIBILITY to SELF * (continued)

losses vary in their impact upon us, our psychic structure varies in its capacity to handle them, and not all of us do it with equal success.

It has been said that the quality which distinguishes a great man from another like him is his capacity to manage disappointment and loss. One thinks of the experiences of Winston Churchill and the crushing disappointments of his early career, or those of Franklin Roosevelt with a disabling onslaught of polio, and begins to realize the wisdom in that observation.

Accepting loss is to accept the reality of it, to allow one's self to feel the pain and anguish of it. One can then come to terms with its meaning to you. Doing so is vital if the spirit is to continue to grow, and in some cases even to survive. It is relevant to note that the successful rehabilitation of a person newly blind, depends upon his first having accepted the painful reality of his loss of vision, in a process of mourning akin to grieving the loss of a loved one.

It brings me to ask: What can you say about your courage to face and to accept the anguish of loss?

V. The fifth query is to ask you to examine the consistency and the quality of your personal relationships. Most of us accept the truism that people are important to people, yet we fail to perceive how often human relationships are superficial, meager and unrewarding. Is this true of your own? Which of your relationships can you say has a quality of involvement with the other, expressing a depth of emotional investment which is real and mutually experienced? It is again too easy to explain that the pressures of our lives and the demands upon us, the superficial materialism of the age and all the rest are what account for a deep sense of poverty in our relationships with others. To call again upon that element of courage to which I earlier referred, can we examine the quality of relationships of those who are closest to us to question how honest, how open, how real they are?

It is clear that the capacity to establish close, significant emotional ties with others is characteristic of emotional maturity. It is clear, moreover, that the work, the effort and sometimes the pain of doing

---

* Roy Menninger, "Responsibility to Self," Menninger Perspective, June/July 1972. Reprinted by permission of the Menninger Foundation.

RESPONSIBILITY to SELF * (continued)

so is quite enough to discourage many, especially when the trends in our society are moving in the same direction. And yet we are still disdainful of the empty superficiality of the cocktail party, even when lessened by the illusion of intimacy which alcohol can provide.

The phenomenon of parallel play in the nursery school—two children in close physical contact with each other but playing entirely alone—is expectable at the age of two or three. When it can be said to characterize a pattern of living at the age of 20 or 40, it hints at relationships eroded by infantile expectations and a lack of mutual commitment. Relationships which show a depth of emotional involvement require a willingness to engage, to share, to listen, to give. What can you say about these qualities in your human relationships?

VI. Not unrelated to a question about your human relationships is a query about sources of your emotional support: From whom do you receive it and to whom do you give it? I have referred to the lack of fulfilling avocation in the lives of many executives—the absence of a rewarding investment in art, in music, in physical activity, in stamp collection or a hundred others. Does this also describe you?

It is also clear that many people who are imbued with an especially strong sense of responsibility have great difficulty in seeking or accepting support from others. For some, this is reminiscent of a profoundly unpleasant sense of helplessness from an earlier phase of life; for some it is an unacceptable admission of weakness, of inadequacy; for some it is a contradiction of one's sense of strength and commitment to help others. Ironically, those whose careers lead to increasing responsibility for others must therefore provide increasing support for others at the very moment when they are progressively more isolated, less able to ask for help for themselves, and less able to receive it when it is available. Greater responsibility generates greater personal need—and greater obstacles to receiving it.

VII. Lastly, any survey of your mental health must ask about the role of love in your lives. For most of us, use of this word threatens a deluge of sentimentality. It is a word which too readily

* Roy Menninger, "Responsibility to Self," Menninger Perspective, June/July 1972. Reprinted by permission of the Menninger Foundation.

RESPONSIBILITY to SELF * (continued)

conjures images of technicolor Hollywood, and cow-eyed adolescents. But it is a respectable feeling. I use it to refer to a capacity to care. Perhaps we are not fully aware that it implies a willingness to invest ourselves in others, to be involved with them, to listen to them —in short, to care about them. It should therefore be a hallmark of all our relationships with others. This is the true sense of helping, for it is the only antidote to hate we know, and is also the foundation stone for that indispensable pillar of good human relationships— trust. Both are always in short supply.

Without intending to promote egocentricity, I would have to ask how truly and how well you love yourself—not in irrational or narcissistic and overblown terms, but as an object of pride and self-esteem, a thing of value, a person of worth. As one can love himself in this mature and realistic way, so he is able to extend the help of love to others in ways which are not demeaning, not controlling, not condescending or patronizing, but respectful and genuinely caring.

Your relationships to others do indeed mirror your relationship to yourself. How well you deal with others may depend upon your success in managing yourself in relation to the provocative and difficult questions I have posed for you today. No one has suggested these questions are easy; in some sense they may be unanswerable. But they do need to be thought about by each of you, talked about with those you love and are close to, and examined repeatedly in the months and years ahead.

* Roy Menninger, "Responsibility to Self," Menninger Perspective, June/July 1972. Reprinted by permission of the Menninger Foundation.

No. 4 — LOVING MY NEIGHBOR AS MYSELF

A. Daily Meditation and Prayer

Use pages on "The Consideration and Practice of Silence" each day as indicated: 1st day, 2nd day, etc., starting tomorrow. Remember to pray daily for your faithful friend.

B. Study:

"Rings and Things"
"Salvation — Fulfillment — Paradoxes"

C. Read and ponder the accountability report of your faithful friend — so that, by the end of the week, having prayed for your friend, you are enabled to make a sensitive written response (which need not be long or detailed).

Prepare your own accountability report for this week—to be given to your faithful friend at your next meeting.

D. Make a daily journal entry. Refresh your mind concerning the uses of your journal. See page 18: "The Keeping of a Journal."

THE CONSIDERATION and PRACTICE OF SILENCE

1st day

". . . the Lord is in his holy temple;
let all the earth keep silence before him." (Habakkuk 2:20 RSV)

"Do you not know that you are God's temple
and that God's Spirit dwells in you? . . .
God's temple is holy, and that temple you are."
(I Cor. 3:16-17 RSV)

"Be still, and know that I am God." (Psalms 46:10 RSV)

"Silence is nothing merely negative; it is not the mere absence of speech. It is a positive, a complete world in itself . . .

There is no beginning to silence and no end: it seems to have its origins in the time when everything was still pure Being. It is like uncreated, everlasting Being . . .

Where silence is, man is observed by silence. Silence looks at man more than man looks at silence. Man does not put silence to the test; silence puts man to the test . . .

Silence is not visible, and yet its existence is clearly apparent. It extends to the farthest distances, yet is so close to us that we can feel it as concretely as we feel our own bodies. It is intangible, yet we can feel it as directly as we feel materials and fabrics. It cannot be defined in words, yet it is quite definite and unmistakable.

In no other phenomenon are distance and nearness, range and immediacy, the all-embracing and the particular, so united as they are in silence.* (pp. 1-2)

---

* Max Picard, The World of Silence, Copyright 1952. Henry Regnery Company. Reprinted by permission of Gateway Editions, Ltd., South Bend, Indiana 46624.

THE CONSIDERATION and PRACTICE OF SILENCE (continued)

2nd day

"The clearly defined and wholly immediate word arises from the indefinite, far-ranging prehistoric realm of silence.

Silence reveals itself in a thousand inexpressible forms: in the quiet of dawn, in the noiseless aspiration of trees towards the sky, in the stealthy descent of night, in the silent changing of the seasons, in the falling moonlight, trickling down into the night like a rain of silence, but above all in the silence of the inward soul . . .

Silence is a world in itself, and from this world of silence speech learns to form itself into a world: the world of silence and the world of speech confront each other . . . One can hear silence sounding through speech. Real speech is in fact nothing but the resonance of silence.* (pp. 10-11)

For MEDITATION: Psalms 19, especially vs. 1-4. Note progression in this Psalm from meditation into prayer.

3rd day

"The present state of the world and the whole of life is diseased. If I were a doctor and were asked for my advice, I should reply: Create silence! Bring men to silence. The Word of God cannot be heard in the noisy world of today. And even if it were blazoned forth with all the panoply of noise so that it could be heard in the midst of all the other noise, then it would no longer be the Word of God. Therefore create silence.* (p. 232)

"It is upon our willingess to listen and hear God speak that our prayer life from first to last depends.** (p. 39)

For MEDITATION: John 10:22-30, especially vs. 27.

4th day — Careless Words

". . . the saints were capable of spiritual silence simply because they had not contracted our modern habit of ceaseless talk in their ordinary life. Their days were days of silence, relieved by periods of conversation, while ours are a wilderness of talk with a rare oasis of silence . . . To put it bluntly, the first step towards attaining interior quiet is to hold one's peace more frequently and to better purpose in the ordinary ways of life.** (p. 49-50)

For MEDITATION: James 3:2-12. (Or Matthew 12:33-37)

---

* Max Picard, The World of Silence, Copyright 1952. Henry Regnery Company. Reprinted by permission of Gateway Editions, Ltd., South Bend, Indiana 46624.

** E. Herman, Creative Prayer. Harper & Row. 1940. Reprinted by permission of Harper & Row, Publishers, Inc.

{off}

THE CONSIDERATION and PRACTICE OF SILENCE (continued)

5th day — Mirrors

". . . it must be borne in mind that the silence we mean is not self-exploration and self-dissection, (nor does it correspond) to the process of psycho-analysis at the hands of an expert. Spiritual silence is the turning of the soul in quietness to a Power beyond itself.* (p. 61)

We shall receive illumination, teaching, and healing, a revelation of truth, by absorbing rather than by analysing.

Quietness

O Thou, the Almighty and Eternal One,
　　Who hast said, 'Be still, and know that I am God,'
let our hearts be to Thee as quiet waters
　　that even in their little depths
　　　　can mirror the eternal stars;
　　　　　　through Jesus Christ, our Lord.　　Amen.

For MEDITATION: Psalm 121.

6th day

". . . the great solitaries always surprise us by their acute understanding of life . . . Prayer of positive, creative quality needs a background of silence, and until we are prepared to practice this silence, we need not hope to know the power of prayer.* (pp. 64-65).

How silently, how silently
The wondrous gift is given.
So God imparts to human hearts
The wonders of His heaven.

". . . it is absurd to talk about interior silence when there is no exterior silence.** (p. 301).

"It is in deep solitude that I find the gentleness with which I can truly love my brothers. The more solitary I am, the more affection I have for them. It is pure affection, and filled with reverence for the solitude of others. Solitude and silence teach me to love my brothers for what they are, not for what they say.** (p. 261).

7th day

For MEDITATION:　　Matthew 22:37-39.

---

* E. Herman, Creative Prayer. Harper & Row. 1940. Reprinted by permission of Harper & Row, Publishers, Inc.
** Thomas Merton, The Sign of Jonas. Copyright, 1953, by The Abbey of Our Lady of Gethsemani. Permission to reprint granted by Harcourt, Brace Jovanovich, Inc.

RINGS AND THINGS *

I am going to divide everyone in the world into two categories: the contemporary American middle class and everyone else. Now, who is everyone else? Well, obviously, the Indians, the primitives, the Asians, the Africans, the poor, the American aristocrats. . . . I am toying with the idea of changing the name from the contemporary "middle class" to the "non-class." . . . What I have discovered is that we are mostly characterized by "not" anything. The first thing that the minority group American has is a name, and a name is prerequisite to his essence of existence . . . Kike, Wop, Nigger, Jew, Dago, Hunkie, Mex, and so on. When I was little, we tried to soften Jew, so we invented the -ishes, and people were not Jews; they were Jewish. So I realized "they" are -ishes.

What I have been asserting is that we have a thing called "contemporary Americans"—you and me, by and large, whom I would like to call the "non-class," and then we have everyone else. This group "We" is sometimes referred to as "The Main Stream," and "They" are not in it.

So now we must think a bit about "Them." I am going to sketch out this dichotomy by means of the word "privacy"—by the idea of privacy. . . . I remember being on a pullman train when the conductor came along and asked me my name. I acted rather angry. My attitude toward his inquiry was, "What's it to you?" A few days later I was on an airplane and the stewardess came along and asked, "What's your name?" I coyly answered, "Howard Higman." There was a difference. "Where am I from?" "Where am I going?" "What do I do?" "What is my name?" "Am I married or not married?" "Do I like my wife?" "What do I intend to do about my wife?" "Which of my children do I fear the most?" These are questions which become more and more private until, finally, we get to the questions of "soul" and "God" and "eternity," and these become very, very private.

---

* Excerpts from "Rings and Things" reprinted by permission of the author, Howard Higman, Professor, Department of Sociology, University of Colorado at Boulder, Colorado.

RINGS AND THINGS * (continued)

On the above left is a diagram intended to describe the contemporary American middle class. The rings represent increasing degrees of privacy. The ring near the center represents a thick barrier. As long as one is on the surface in the contemporary American middle class, the material is acceptable to anybody. But one runs into an impermeable barrier as he gets near the center. Thus, there is a very great deal of accessible information about the individual in the American middle class until one gets to the inner impermeable barrier.

On the other hand, as shown in the diagram on the right, the minority group member has a barrier near the outer surface, so there is very little material to which one has immediate access. One bumps into the barrier almost immediately. But there is another fact about his barrier. It is not as thick or as strong as the one in the middle-class ring-set. If one does succeed in getting through it, one is through it all the way.

Each ring in the diagram on the left represents an increasing degree of privateness. In the diagram on the right, which is not the contemporary American middle class, either because it is not contemporary, or it is not middle, or it is not American, the hypothesis is that the privacy barrier is near the surface. In the contemporary American middle class the barrier is near the center. That's one of two points.

---

* Excerpts from "Rings and Things" reprinted by permission of the author, Howard Higman, Professor, Department of Sociology, University of Colorado at Boulder, Colorado.

RINGS AND THINGS * (continued)

The other point is that the barrier in the contemporary American middle class is impermeable. You cannot get through it. In the minority group, it is permeable. It is near the surface, but it is nowhere as thick.

Now we look at the condition in which two people come together. My word for this is proximity. Two persons . . . they are sitting in the waiting room outside of the emergency ward of a hospital. They are in proximity. If the two persons are members of the middle class, even though strangers, they will be acceptable to each other. If, on the other hand, they are members of a minority group, the barrier between them is right at the surface and the difference between relationships is quite apparent, as one can discover by listening to their conversations and noting the things that these people tell each other as they pass the time.

There is a phenomenon among minority group individuals which is not found in the middle class. When a member of a minority group calls another individual "friend," it means that he and the other individual have crossed each other's barrier and have shared their souls with each other. They have no barrier between them and their relationship to each other is that of friends. When one looks at the diagram on the left and thinks about it, one may deduce from it that persons in the middle class really have no friends. This is the principal idea that I am trying to get across—that membership in the contemporary middle class deprives one of friends. The word "friend" may be used, but such friends do not fulfill that role by lower-class standards. If one is very observant, he will notice that in the diagrams of the middle class there is no difference between so-called friends and mere proximities. Members of the American middle class have no close friends—they obviously run into the inner barrier and stop.

The word I use for this middle class pseudo friendship is "ally." What members of the middle class have are allies or alliances. They have to have alliances to survive in dangerous American society. For instance, any girl who lives in a dormitory or sorority house will not receive telephone messages if she does not have an ally. The phone in the hall rings and a non-ally answers and says, "Hello. Sorry, she's not here," and hangs up. But if the ally answers, she says, "Charlotte's here. Just a minute, I'll call her." And if Charlotte is not in, she returns to the phone and tells the caller, "Gee, she was here a minute ago. Can I tell her who's calling? Oh, Chris. All right, I'll tell her." And the message gets to Charlotte.

* Excerpts from "Rings and Things" reprinted by permission of the author, Howard Higman, Professor, Department of Sociology, University of Colorado at Boulder, Colorado.

RINGS AND THINGS * (continued)

The important thing is that this relationship, which you think of as a friendship, is actually sustained by the situation—the field situation. In the absence of a field situation, the relationship of friendship breaks down for the American middle-class person. Persons in the middle class mistake alliances for friendships. They are not. One test of this process is to look at a Christmas card list that is five years old: what one sees is a list of then-current allies. And these "lifelong friends" of the past we have somehow lost track of. There is no continuity in alliance systems, except those directly correlated with one's staying-put in the same set system.

* Excerpts from "Rings and Things" reprinted by permission of the author, Howard Higman, Professor, Department of Sociology, University of Colorado at Boulder, Colorado.

SALVATION — FULFILLMENT — PARADOXES

* What everyman looks for in life is his own salvation and the salvation of the men he lives with. By salvation I mean first of all the full discovery of who he himself really is. Then I mean something of the fulfillment of his own God-given powers, in the love of others and of God. I mean also the discovery that he cannot find himself in himself alone, but that he must find himself in and through others. Ultimately, these propositions are summed up in two lines of the Gospel: "If any man would save his life, he must lose it," and, "Love one another as I have loved you." It is also contained in another saying from St. Paul: "We are all members one of another."

The salvation I speak of is not merely a subjective, psychological thing—a self-realization in the order of nature. It is an objective and mystical reality—the finding of ourselves in Christ, in the Spirit, or, if you prefer, in the supernatural order. This includes and sublimates and perfects the natural self-realization which it to some extent presupposes, and usually effects, and always transcends. Therefore this discovery of ourselves is always a losing of ourselves—a death and a resurrection. "Your life is hidden with Christ in God." The discovery of ourselves in God, and of God in ourselves, by a charity that also finds all other men in God with ourselves is, therefore, not the discovery of ourselves but of Christ. First of all, it is the realization that "I live; yet not I, but Christ liveth in me," and secondly it is the penetration of that tremendous mystery which St. Paul sketched out boldly—and darkly—in his great Epistles: the mystery of the recapitulation, the summing up of all in Christ. It is to see the world in Christ, its beginning and its end. To see all things coming forth from God in the Logos Who becomes incarnate and descends into the lowest depths of His own creation and gathers all to Himself in order to restore it finally to the Father at the end of time. To find "ourselves" then is to find not only our poor, limited, perplexed souls, but to find the power of God that raised Christ from the dead and "built us together in Him unto a habitation of God in the Spirit" (Ephesians 2:22).

This discovery of Christ is never genuine if it is nothing but a flight from ourselves. On the contrary, it cannot be an escape. It must be a fulfillment. I cannot discover God in myself and myself in Him unless I have the courage to face myself exactly as I am, with all my limitations, and to accept others as they are, with all their limitations. The religious answer is not religious if it is not fully real. Evasion is the answer of superstition.

---

* This page is from No Man is An Island by Thomas Merton. Copyright (c) 1955 by The Abbey of Our Lady of Gethsemani. Reprinted by permission of Harcourt, Brace, Jovanovich, Inc. (pp. 14-16).

SALVATION — FULFILLMENT — PARADOXES (continued)

This matter of "salvation" is, when seen intuitively, a very simple thing. But when we analyze it, it turns into a complex tangle of paradoxes. We become ourselves by dying to ourselves. We gain only what we give up, and if we give up everything we gain everything. We cannot find ourselves within ourselves, but only in others, yet at the same time before we can go out to others we must first find ourselves. We must forget ourselves in order to become truly conscious of who we are. The best way to love ourselves is to love others, yet we cannot love others unless we love ourselves since it is written, "Thou shalt love they neighbor as thyself." But if we love ourselves in the wrong way, we become incapable of loving anybody else. And indeed when we love ourselves wrongly we hate ourselves; if we hate ourselves we cannot help hating others. Yet there is a sense in which we must hate others and leave them in order to find God. Jesus said: "If any man come to me and hate not his father and his mother . . . yea and his own life also, he cannot be my disciple" (Luke 14:26). As for this "finding" of God, we cannot even look for Him unless we have already found him, and we cannot find Him unless He has first found us. We cannot begin to seek Him without a special gift of His grace, yet if we wait for grace to move us, before beginning to seek Him, we will probably never begin.

The only effective answer to the problem of salvation must therefore reach out to embrace both extremes of a contradiction at the same time. Hence that answer must be supernatural. That is why all the answers that are not supernatural are imperfect: for they only embrace one of the contradictory terms, and they can always be denied by the other.*

---

* This page is from No Man Is An Island by Thomas Merton. Copyright (c) 1955, by The Abbey of our Lady of Gethsemani. Reprinted by permission of Harcourt, Brace, Jovanovich, Inc. (pp. 14-16).

No. 5 — REVIEW

1st day

Review all papers in Section NO. 1—Having The Faithful Friend

MEDITATE on: Rev. 3:20. . . . Have you "opened the door"?

2nd day

Review papers included in NO. 2—Becoming a faithful friend.

MEDITATE on: (We) "ought always to pray and not lose heart."
(Luke 18:1 RSV)

Are there parts of the process of becoming a faithful friend that:
— you have found particularly helpful?
— you feel you need to clarify? Or to have clarified?
— you find yourself resisting?

3rd day

Review papers included in NO. 3—I must love myself.

MEDITATE on: "You shall love your neighbor as yourself."
(Matt. 22:39 RSV)

Ponder your answers to Questions I, II, III, and IV in paper by Dr. Roy Menninger.

4th day

Continue review of NO. 3

Ponder your answers to Questions V, VI and VII of Menninger paper.

No. 5 — REVIEW (continued)

5th day

Review papers included in NO. 4.

Do you see a relationship between the diagram of yourself (on the page "Ring of Yourself") with "i am" as the smallest ring—and the diagram on the left side of the paper on "Rings and Things?"

What has the process of developing faithful friendship to do with these diagrams?

6th day

Review your journal entries—and jot down:

— One of your satisfying insights from study, meditation, prayer.
— Your questions about assignments.
— Anything you might wish to share with your faithful friend.
— Ideas about topics it would be helpful to pursue.
— Ways the concept of faithful friendship could be adapted in varying situations.

7th day

MEDITATE on: ". . . whatsover a man sows, that he will also reap."
(Gal. 6:7 RSV)

"Thou openest thy hand, thou satisfiest the desire of every living thing." (Ps. 145:16 RSV)

No. 6 — GOD — THE GIVER OF EVERY GIFT

<u>DAILY</u> — <u>Pray</u> for your faithful friend.
   <u>Make entry</u> in your journal.

<u>1st day</u>

— <u>MEDITATE</u> and pray Psalm 145 (Note the four "I-Thee" prayer passages, the four meditative passages, and the final 'resolution.')

— <u>Read and carefully consider</u> your faithful friend's accountability report.

<u>2nd day</u>

— <u>Study page:</u> "God is the Giver of Every Gift."
— <u>Read Luke 15:11-32</u>, and <u>meditate</u> on any part of it that speaks especially to you.

<u>3rd</u>
<u>4th</u>
<u>5th</u>
<u>6th days</u>

— <u>Continue to study page</u> on "GIFT — God is The Giver of Every Gift."
— Read over "One Method of Meditation."

 <u>Try using this method</u> at least once — or use that part of it that is helpful to you.

 Each day you could PICTURE yourself as a different participant in this parable — as the elder son, the father, the prodigal son, a servant, an invited guest. (Luke 15:11-32)

 Methods are suggested merely to help you to discover what is good and right for you. Regimented meditating and praying with a set method can defeat spontaneous prayer.

PARADOX: Using a method of meditation is helpful as a gateway to prayer.
   Using a method of meditation defeats spontaneous prayer.

<u>7th day</u>

— <u>Continue to study and to meditate and pray.</u>
— <u>Prepare your accountability report.</u>
— <u>Write your response</u> to your faithful friend's accountability report.

One METHOD of MEDITATION — from MAKING PRAYER REAL *

Familiarity with the enriching forms of mental prayer that have been used by Christian leaders down through the centuries will aid us in making our prayer-life more God-centered. There are five essential parts to the classic devotional practices to which five appropriate names have been given. Their alliteration makes them easy to remember: prepare, picture, ponder, promise, pray.

PREPARE—Our remote preparation comes from the background of sincere Christian living from which all real prayer must rise. We must never forget that we are constantly preparing for prayer by the way we live our daily life.

Our proximate preparation begins the night before. We read our Bible in accordance with some planned sequence, and then select a verse or a phrase as the subject on which we will meditate the next morning. Any incident or teaching in the life of Christ might be chosen—or the attributes of God; the great Christian virtues, the Lord's Prayer, the Beatitudes, the Ten Commandments . . . Then:

Our immediate preparation includes;

   a. Stillness—We let the mind repose a little until we grow silent, considering how God is looking at us and inviting us into the secret place of the Most High.

   b. Recollection—We center our hearts on God. "We are kneeling before a great Personality without form but having an intensely personal love which surrounds us." This should be for us a fact of conviction even before it is a fact of consciousness.

   c. Confession (Awareness)—Instinctively we sense our unworthiness to kneel in the Presence of God. We evidence the sincerity of our desire to commune with Him by expressing penitence for all sins that disturb our relationship to Him.

   d. Invocation—We ask God to help us as we pray. We offer to Him our minds, our affections, our wills. We ask grace to deepen our spiritual attention. We repeat:

     "Spirit of God, descend upon my heart;
     Wean it from earth; through all its pulses move;
     Stoop to my weakness, mighty as Thou art;
     And make me love Thee as I ought to love." (George Croly)

* From MAKING PRAYER REAL by Lynn James Radcliffe. Copyright 1952 by Pierce and Smith. Used by permission of Abingdon. (pp. 132-143)

One METHOD of MEDITATION—from MAKING PRAYER REAL* (cont.)

PICTURE—We now recall the subject which we are to consider, and set it before us with the aid of our imagination. There is a distinction that should be clearly recognized between fancy and creative imagination. Fancy is the power to picture something regardless of whether or not it is true. Creative imagination enables us to picture vividly and vitally something known to be true. The use of creative imagination in meditation will make the truth considered come alive for us, stimulate our minds to think, and prepare our hearts and wills for active response . . . We consider the event as though the action were being performed in our presence . . . We use sensory images as a starting point to enable us to go beyond them.

PONDER — We now turn the full power of our thought upon the scene asking that it yield to us its meaning. We can prod our minds with questions, asking Who? Where? Why? How? When? For Whom? By what aids? With what love? OR: What do I know about it? What do I think about it? What can I do about it? OR: What does this truth mean to me? It is well for us to keep in mind a particular virtue of which we stand in need. As we thus ponder about some vital truth, life deepens into real communion with God.

PROMISE — No prayer is true prayer until it issues in an act of response. Prayer is not a golden glow or a purple mood. It is the achievement of such a oneness with the Spirit of God as impels us at any cost to adjust our daily living to the level of His high purposes for us and to clear from our consciousness every hidden barrier that impedes the flow of God's power through us.

First, there should be a general resolution to give ourselves entirely to God in all things today. With a profound distrust of ourselves, but with utter confidence in Him, we make this general oblation of our lives.

---

* From MAKING PRAYER REAL by Lynn James Radcliffe. Copyright 1952 by Pierce and Smith. Used by permission of Abingdon. (pp. 132-143)

One METHOD of MEDITATION—from MAKING PRAYER REAL * (cont.)

But the climax of the promises which we make comes in one or more definite resolutions. These should be as particular as we can possibly make them—something definite, something to be done today, even at a particular time. Such as:

Solemnly to hand over to God's keeping one small fear.
An attempt to make one half-hour of work during the day a special vehicle for God's power.
To endeavor to pass a whole day without making one excuse.
To get through the day without a grumble.
Intentionally to copy one of Christ's actions during the day.

PRAY — There should always come a time when we slowly shift our gaze from the subject considered to God, by whose grace we have been meditating. We pass into a spontaneous form of prayer, informal and intimate—the colloquy—which is the normal way of prayer for all of us. Our colloquy is free and unplanned. Petitions are offered. We ask grace to put into practice our promises and to keep our resolutions. We seek victory over temptation, especially our ruling temptation. We ask for "personal interior knowledge of our Lord that we may love Him more dearly and follow Him more nearly." But what will unite us to God? Not merely our good thoughts but the good movement of our wills and affections is needed. We offer up intercession for many others. We use acts of devotion that rise unbidden from our hearts to express our praise, love, homage, and faith. We LISTEN for His word to us.

As we practice the art of mental prayer, there will come times when our hearts will be drawn directly toward God. Feelings will surge up out of the deeps of us in response to Him whom we have glimpsed in our meditation. Fired by the love of God, we shall then leave our considerations and our methods and respond in spontaneous and fervent outpourings of adoration, praise, and love.

* From MAKING PRAYER REAL by Lynn James Radcliffe. Copyright 1952 by Pierce and Smith. Used by permission of Abingdon. (pp. 132-143)

God — as Giver of all gifts.
Ourselves — as recipients of gift.
Ourselves — as givers of gifts, by
the grace of God

GOD IS THE GIVER OF EVERY GIFT

A. God, who is Life, Love, and Light—gives to us life, love, light. God, who in Christ showed himself to be self-giving Love, offers to be present and to manifest himself in each of us. This is his gift.

A gift is not just a handing-over of a material thing or a talent from one to another. Any gift is in some way a giving of oneself. "The gift without the giver is bare." Both the giver and the recipient are implicitly aware of this.

B. God did not give his only begotten Son on condition that the Son be treated well and accepted by men. He does not love us only when we are righteous. His light shines on the just and the unjust.

A gift is unconditional. There are "no strings attached." The giver has no premeditated intention of securing a hold over the recipient because of the recipient's gratitude for the gift. The recipient is not intended by the giver to feel obligation. (See Menninger paper, "love . . . in ways which are not demeaning, not controlling, not condescending or patronizing . . .")

Note: Many of the thoughts on this page are taken from Gabriel Marcel: The Mystery of Being, Vol. II, pp. 132-134. Copyright 1960, Gateway Edition, Henry Regnery Company. Reprinted by permission of Gateway Editions, Ltd., South Bend, Indiana 46624.

GOD IS THE GIVER OF EVERY GIFT   (continued)

C. God, in giving himself to us, in being present and manifesting himself, extends himself. Thus he enables us, by the giving of ourselves to others, to manifest his Presence to others and so to extend the area of his self-giving love—to extend his Kingdom.

To give is to expand, to extend. It is not as though a gift were an overflow of something that is too full—but rather it is the result of generosity. And generosity seems always to include an element of sacrifice "well mixed with joy."

Generosity is to be carefully distinguished from prodigality. Prodigality is lavish, unwise, extravagant.
Generosity may be defined as "a light whose joy is in giving light, in being light."

The term 'light' provides a way of interpreting experiences as different as those of the artist, the hero, or the saint. 'Radiance' is the only word which can express these experiences, and this radiance emanates from the giver himself as well as from his gift.

Joy is not complacent self-satisfaction. It is not a satisfaction; it is an exaltation.

Note: Many of the thoughts on this page are taken from Gabriel Marcel: The Mystery of Being, Vol. II, pp. 132-134. Copyright 1960, Gateway Edition, Henry Regnery Company. Reprinted by permission of Gateway Editions, Ltd., South Bend, Indiana 46624.

No. 7 — OURSELVES AS RECIPIENTS OF GOD'S GIFTS

N.B. This week's study and materials offer opportunity for you to exercise maturity in choosing daily for yourself the portion of the materials best suited for your meditation.

DAILY — Pray for your faithful friend.
   Make entry in your journal.

   Study: Pages entitled "Ourselves as Recipients of God's Gifts."
   Each day choose a paragraph from the study pages that appeals to you, meditate on it and on one of the suggested Scriptures or on another pertinent Scripture passage of your own choosing.

Prepare your accountability report.

Write response to your faithful friend's accountability report.

   "If a man wills to obey God's will,
      he is already obeying it.
   But let there be no humbug about this.
   To say merely 'I want' relates to a future thing;
      it must be 'I will, by God's grace,'
      and this ensures possession of the present moment.*
                                                      (p. 200)

   "To think of penance as giving up and not as giving
      is to look too much at the deprivations
         and not enough at Him for Whom
            the deprivations are made.*
                                                      (p. 229)

---

*APPROACH TO PENANCE and APPROACH TO PRAYER by Hubert Van Zeller, Copyright 1958, Sheed & Ward, Inc., New York.

OURSELVES AS RECIPIENTS OF GOD'S GIFTS (continued)

A. Attitude of "waiting on the Lord". This is requisite.

Rufus Jones says that the search for God is a two-way search. God is searching for us, but it is necessary that we be in search of him. Having found us, God cannot give us the gift of Himself unless we are prepared to receive it. God Himself cannot place his gift in a clenched fist.

1. ". . . the scriptural phrase . . . 'waiting on the Lord' is poignantly rich today. We need as never before to keep a place in the order of life for God to act. If we rush in and take over, filling the place with human busyness, we shut Him out. We do not win His peace. It is in this sense that peace is the power of receptivity. It is in essence the waiting for God to act, knowing that no matter how much we may act, no matter how strenuously or how tirelessly, we can never substitute our action for God's action.

   We seek then to practice what we often know, that there are many things which will come to us only as gifts and never by our attempt to earn them. . . . Simone Weil . . . says, 'We do not obtain the most precious gifts by going in search of them but by waiting for them.'

   It would almost seem as if this forces man into a negative role, yet this is farthest from the truth. The peace that comes from withdrawing oneself is totally different from the peace which makes oneself available to God. Waiting for God is a sublime activity, but it is not strenuous straining. It is the point at which receptivity or openness becomes more than a mere invitation. It is, in Marcel's word, an invocation. It is the appropriately humble response of finite man to the grace of God's infinite power." (p. 166-7)

   Suggested MEDITATION: Psalm 27, esp. vs. 14.

---

* Samuel H. Miller, The Great Realities, Copyright 1955 by Harper & Row, Publishers, Inc. Reprinted by permission of the publisher.

OURSELVES AS RECIPIENTS OF GOD'S GIFTS (continued)

2. "To wait well, to make oneself really available is the most positive of work . . . It is not sheer strenuosity so much beloved by moderns. It isn't straining with muscles and nerve taut. This kind of spiritual work may be termed openness. It is the opposite of the tight, tense mood which is nearer fear than love. It is born of faith, the assurance of things hoped for, of things unseen, and is attended by all the powers of creation. For this kind of openness is creative. It is the openness of poets, scientists, and musicians who seek to serve the greater glory by their waiting and listening and brooding. Not by will, thrusting itself against the world, but by faith which opens the doors from the inside and invites the visit of the All High do we acknowledge God's prior action. Not by might of pressure or incessant activity but by a thousand motions of the imagination, the cleansing by repentance, the humility of surrender does the soul reconcile itself to God . . . it takes a tremendous amount of imagination, of repentance, of deeper and deeper humility to deepen ourselves down to that simple level at which He serves and sustains our life.* (pp. 60-61)

3. " 'The occasion and the experience . . . are nothing. It all depends on the capacity of the soul to be grasped.' It is this 'being grasped' which carries us again to the open faith in God's loving power, a faith which continues into the darkness and confusion of experiences hard to endure or to understand but in which one still expects to see the hand of God moving in its ministry of grace and redemption.* (p. 173)

MEDITATION: I Samuel 3: 2-10, Mark 1: 16-20, John 1:35-49, Luke 18: 15-30

---

* Samuel H. Miller, The Great Realities, Copyright 1955 by Harper & Row, Publishers, Inc. Reprinted by permission of the publisher.

OURSELVES AS RECIPIENTS OF GOD'S GIFTS (continued)

B. Repentance: Obedience and Penance

Note: The following excerpts all stress the same thing. This is interesting, coming as the excerpts do, from the following authors:

John B. Coburn,
  Bishop of the Episcopal Diocese of Massachusetts
Abraham Joshua Heschel,
  Rabbi, former Professor at Jewish Theological Seminary
Morton Kelsey, Jungian psychologist, Episcopal minister
Hubert van Zeller, Order of St. Benedict
Donald M. Baillie,
  former Professor at University of St. Andrew

1. "... love ... is hard work, sacrificial work. It is carried out by people willing to give up having their own way so that love may have its way.* (p. 31)

"We are in fact sinners, and it is only honest to confess our sins. But we are also recipients of grace, and we should confirm those graces we have been given, as well as confess the sins we have committed. The church needs a service parallel to the Sacrament of Penance that might be called the Sacrament of Grace, in which the recipient of grace would acknowledge, 'Through no virtue of my own, I have received a letter from a friend, a handshake from a former enemy, an unexpected kiss, a lift to my spirit when a dove called another dove, a sense of awe when I saw the moon rise, and joy when the heavens flicked their lights across the darkness.'

The essential fact about us is not that we are sinners, but receivers of grace. And we need to remind ourselves of this.

Identify the graces that come to you. Give them as you can. In the grace of giving, you give yourself.* (pp. 97-97).

MEDITATION: Ephesians 2: 1-10

2. "Life is tangled, fierce, fickle. We cannot remain in agreement with all goals. We are constantly compelled to make a choice, and the choice of one goal means the forsaking of another.** (p. 106). MEDITATION: Matthew 7: 24.

---

* John B. Coburn, A Life to Live—A Way to Pray, Copyright (c) 1973 by John B. Coburn. Seabury Press. Reprinted by permission of John B. Coburn.
** Abraham Joshua Heschel, Man Is Not Alone, Copyright 1951 by Abraham Joshua Heschel. Reprinted by permission of Farrar, Straus & Giroux, Inc., Book Publishers.

OURSELVES AS RECIPIENTS OF GOD'S GIFTS (continued)

3. "Jesus . . . spoke of achieving the single eye, implying that human beings could be other than single-eyed, single-minded —that there might be various centers of personality, as well as more than one way of centering or orienting the self. He spoke again and again—it is almost the keynote of the Gospels—of losing one's life in order to find it. Whatever else this means, it certainly implies that there are various levels of personality, and that to gain one of them another has to be sacrificed. The importance of these concepts can hardly be overestimated in seeking an understanding of Jesus and the New Testament. One has to give up one's own will so that God's will, God's Spirit, the Holy Spirit can become the center of one's life and person-ality.* (p. 64)

   MEDITATION: Matthew 6: 22-23; John 6: 38.

4. "Penance is giving up one form of activity in order to allow greater play to another form of activity. This will is not pri-marily an agent of rebellion, the heart is not primarily a source of temptation. Once it is grasped that these powers are created essentially God-centred, the question is not so much how to curb their activity as how to canalize it—how to develop and direct their appetite towards God . . . The principle of all Christian penance is response to grace . . . self-indulgence cannot go hand in hand with full discipleship of Christ . . . But before the significant decision is made, there is normally great conflict.** MEDITATION: Luke 9: 23-25.

5. ". . . I would tell a tale of God calling His human children to form a great circle for the playing of His game. In that circle we ought all to be standing, linked together with lovingly joined hands, facing towards the Light in the centre, which is God ('the Love that moves the sun and the other stars'); seeing our fellow creatures all round the circle in the light of that central Love, which shines on them and beautifies their faces; and joining with them in the dance of God's great game, the rhythm of love universal. But instead of that, we have, each one, turned our backs upon God and the circle of our fellows, and faced the other way, so that we can see neither the Light at the centre nor the faces on the circumference. And indeed in that

   * * *

* Morton T. Kelsey, Healing and Christianity, Copyright (c) 1973, Morton T. Kelsey. Harper & Row, Publishers, Inc. Reprinted by permission of Morton T. Kelsey.

** APPROACH TO PENANCE and APPROACH TO PRAYER by Hubert Van Zeller, Copyright 1958, Sheed & Ward, Inc., New York.

*** D. M. Baillie, God Was in Christ, Copyright, 1948, by Charles Scribner's Sons. Reprinted by permission of publisher. (pp. 205-6).

OURSELVES AS RECIPIENTS OF GOD'S GIFTS (continued)

position it is difficult even to join hands with our fellows! Therefore instead of playing God's game we play, each one, our own selfish little game, like the perverse children Jesus saw in the market-place, who would not join in the dance with their companions. Each one of us wishes to be the centre, and there is blind confusion, and not even any true knowledge of God or of our neighbors. That is what is wrong with mankind. Of course a man is not really happy in that attitude and situation, since he was created for community with God and man. Moreover, the light of God is still shining from the true centre upon his back, though not on his face. It throws his own shadow on the ground in front of him, and the shadow is contorted into grotesque shapes with every movement that he makes, until his whole world looks queer and unfriendly (it is indeed a fallen world, a ruined world). He knows, dimly or clearly, that all is not well. Perhaps he tries to make himself happy by pursuing his dance more furiously, but then his shadow dances still more mockingly, and things are worse than ever. For, as moralists have so often said, the quest of happiness defeats itself. Perhaps he even tries to mend matters by making himself good. But again he does not succeed. For, though this is not so obvious to moralists, the quest of goodness also defeats itself. The whole procedure of trying to improve our own characters keeps us thinking about ourselves. It is self-centered, and self-centredness is the very thing from which we need to be saved, because it is the essence of sin. That method fails, and failure brings discouragement and moral paralysis. Or, if we ever begin to succeed in improving ourselves, or even to think we are succeeding, then we congratulate ourselves secretly on our achievement, which is the very worst kind of self-centredness—self-righteousness and pride. So instead of becoming saints, we become 'Pharisees.' *

---

6. "To give up seems to be the only sin God cannot do anything about.** (p. 63)

   "Life is what happens to us when we're making other plans. **
   (p. 81)

   ". . . the bearing of . . . conflicts . . . with grace, and if possible with humor, is the mark of the mature, growing human being.**
   (p. 82)

   ". . . we look at him and listen to him to discover what he wants us to know about his life and death, and so about ours.** (p. 91)

---

* D. M. Baillie, God Was in Christ, Copyright, 1948, by Charles Scribner's Sons. Reprinted by permission of publisher. (pp. 205-6).
** John B. Coburn, A Life to Live—A Way to Pray, Copyright (c) 1973 by John B. Coburn, Seabury Press. Reprinted by permission of John B. Coburn.

No. 8 — WE, AS RECIPIENTS, BECOME GIVERS

Withdrawal for quiet time of meditation, prayer, and journaling should be consistent and should become habitual—not, however, with rigid inflexibility when there is valid reason for interruption or variation.

A. Maintain all disciplines.

Meditate each day this week on Luke 8:1-21, using the page "Hearing the Word of God."

Pray — always including listening to your Faithful Friend on behalf of your faithful friend.

B. Peruse (read with care—study—absorb) the paper "Encounter with God."

Remember Christ's injunction: "Love one another as I have loved you."
We, as recipients, become givers.

N.B. Our daily lives offer hour-by-hour, sometimes moment-by-moment opportunity to be friend to others as He is Friend to us.

HEARING the WORD of GOD

No one can be a faithful friend to <u>anyone</u> without being able to hear
—to listen with fixed attention.

SCRIPTURE for MEDITATION: LUKE 8: 1-21

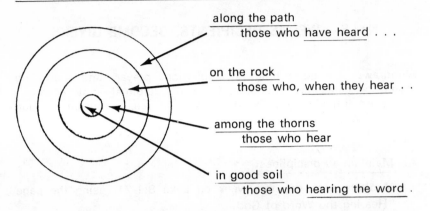

along the path
    those who <u>have heard</u> . . .

on the rock
    those who, <u>when they hear</u> . .

among the thorns
    those who hear

in good soil
    those who <u>hearing the word</u> .

In a spiritual 'sense'—all the senses—hearing, seeing, touching,
tasting, and smelling—mean the same thing:

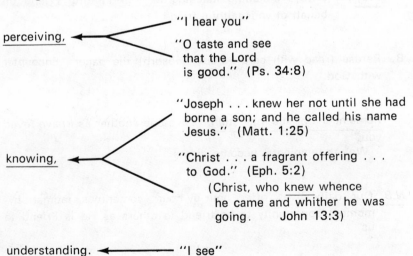

<u>perceiving,</u>

    "I hear you"

    "O taste and see
    that the Lord
    is good." (Ps. 34:8)

    "Joseph . . . knew her not until she had
    borne a son; and he called his name
    Jesus." (Matt. 1:25)

<u>knowing,</u>

    "Christ . . . a fragrant offering . . .
    to God." (Eph. 5:2)

      (Christ, who <u>knew</u> whence
      he came and whither he was
      going. John 13:3)

<u>understanding.</u>   "I see"

How does the Word of God come to you? How does God speak? How
do you hear the Word of God? <u>List as many ways as you can.</u>

Do you truly listen to your Faithful Friend in order to hear the Word
for your faithful friend? And do you truly listen to your faithful
friend to hear the Word that may be spoken through him/her for
you?

ENCOUNTER WITH GOD *

One of the cardinal principles of Christianity is that what we have received freely, we should give freely . . . Wherever Christianity has been alive and creative we find this same emphasis. Putting love into action is the one significant way we human beings are given to express our gratitude, and like humility, gratitude is the rock bottom foundation for every rule for the spiritual encounter.

The importance of love is central in the teaching and, even more significantly, in the life of Jesus. In Paul's writings—who, like Peter, felt that love covers a multitude of sins—the word love may be substituted anywhere for the Holy Spirit with little change in meaning; it is the action which most nearly characterizes the Holy Spirit . . . Agnes Sanford writes that love is the essential quality of the healing power which operates through the Christian.

If this is true, then what are we to understand from it? Why should the outer actions of our lives have such an influence upon our capacity to confront the inner realm and experience it? Principally this is because the inner realities are different from the outer ones. They are not governed by mechanical laws, even to any degree, and for this reason they do not reveal their deepest meanings indiscriminately to everyone who searches. God, who is at the heart and center of psychic reality, is never pressed into confrontation; rather he gives of himself when and where he will. Nor can the approach to the spiritual realm be made with just the mind and consciousness. It involves the total psyche—hence the extreme importance of honesty —and love conditions the nature of the psyche, shaping it into the kind of instrument which is able to deal with the realm of the spirit. The door to the center of this realm is love, and we do not find it unless our lives are turned in that direction. It is as if we approached this door, which is love, each one with a key which he has been required to shape out of his own life, and if it does not fit, the door will not open.

---

* Reprinted by permission from ENCOUNTER WITH GOD by Morton Kelsey, published and copyright 1972, Bethany Fellowship, Inc., Minneapolis, Minnesota 55438. (pp. 200-205)

64

ENCOUNTER WITH GOD * (continued)

Our need to manifest love outwardly has several important corollaries: For one, the person who has made the divine confrontation can no longer live entirely for himself. He must become involved in the world, although not by taking all its burdens upon his heart. This would destroy any man. Rather he must, as the Quakers put it, find his concern, some kind of social action. This is requisite if a man's spiritual life is to continue. Indeed the continuing confrontation of the divine depends upon the sincerity and integrity with which he turns outward to share what he has found. One may enter the realm of the spirit, find the richest experiences within it, receive power which is startling and real, and still be cut off completely from that life and power if he fails to turn outward and express it.

There are dangers of falling into the brand of social action we label "do-goodism," but they are much less when we are honestly aware how much it means to us to relate to the spiritual world. Doing good loses its punch only if it is taken over by ego motives instead of springing from divine inspiration, or when it becomes such a central concern that there is no time left over for the divine encounter. The surest test is when it begins to make us irritable with our families or co-workers. Then it is time to take a good look at what we are doing, remembering that doing good is not what gets us into the kingdom of heaven; and neither does avoiding it.

Another corollary of love is our need to practice listening. By this I mean the forgotten art of listening in which one empties himself and lets the totality of another personality make an impact upon his inmost being. As one discovers the totality of the other human psyche which confronts him, he can come to know the Holy Spirit which dwells and moves in the depth of the other person's soul. One can thus come to a divine encounter through another person's soul by listening. In real listening it is because we love and want the other person to be what he is; we listen to him as God listens lovingly to us.

. . . there is a difference between this kind of compassionate, loving listening, and listening with indifference, and the person talking can sense it. A story is told from one minister's sanctum which I can vouch is too true to be fiction. A man he had been counseling came in one day and sat down and did not have a word to say.

* Reprinted by permission from ENCOUNTER WITH GOD by Morton Kelsey, published and copyright 1972, Bethany Fellowship, Inc., Minneapolis, Minnesota 55438. (pp. 200-205)

ENCOUNTER WITH GOD * (continued)

There he sat for the whole hour, and when he finally got up to leave, he said to the minister, "You will never know what this has meant to me. I didn't think there was any man on earth who could stand me for an hour without saying a word." This kind of listening is not easy; it must be learned, and even then it is one of the most exhausting activities a person can undertake—demanding the total psyche—and one of the most rewarding. Actually I have found out more about God through the people who have come to talk with me than from any amount of reading. In this kind of listening one does not find it necessary to make the other person over, and through it one participates in depth of another's being, and so in the spiritual world on which his life is based.

A third corollary of practicing love is involvement in fellowship or community. This word has been spread so thin that it has come to mean a superficial kind of human relating, almost a game of keeping up pretenses. Real fellowship is anything but this. In genuine fellowship with another person in a small group (two is merely the smallest group) there is an interaction of one total person with another, without the need of pretenses or masks, in an atmosphere of acceptance and love. And, in return, acceptance and love grow out of the interaction. If this kind of give and take between real people is to be possible, rather than the meeting of masks which is all that happens in most groups, a man must know that he can let down his mask. Before one can be himself, revealing what he considers are the less attractive aspects of himself, he must know that he will be accepted and not put on display, that he can be loved just as he is.

Out of this meeting of person with person there will be conflict and disagreement. So often Christians believe that human relationships should be devoid of conflict, yet there can be no genuine meeting of person with person without friction. Jesus never suggested that there should be no conflict among human beings—only no unresolved conflicts. In fact, those who run their lives so that they avoid all conflict with other people also avoid love and real fellowship. These simply do not grow outside of total contact with another person, and this is bound to involve conflict. Love comes out of action, not ideas or thought. And action involves concrete contact and relationship . . .

---

* Reprinted by permission from ENCOUNTER WITH GOD by Morton Kelsey, published and copyright 1972, Bethany Fellowship, Inc., Minneapolis, Minnesota 55438. (pp. 200-205)

ENCOUNTER WITH GOD * (continued)

Churches ought to be the place where one could find real fellow-ship and relationship; yet for most people they are the last place where one expects to find—or to give—it. The real person is revealed far more in the meat market and the beauty shop than in church. In church we try to be what we think we ought to be, and the other person does the same, and how utterly unreal the meeting is. There are a few churches, however, which have begun to experiment with small groups, meeting to study and discuss the basic issues of life. This kind of encounter with other human beings brings about real relationship as these people meet week after week. There is conflict and then real love . . .

Youth today are crying out against the lack of love and concern which is obvious not only in our secular society but in our churches as well. If our young people who most need the church are to be reached, it must be with a message of real love, well integrated and under-stood.

* Reprinted by permission from ENCOUNTER WITH GOD by Morton Kelsey, pub-lished and copyright 1972, Bethany Fellowship, Inc., Minneapolis, Minnesota 55438. (pp. 200-205)

No. 9 — PERSEVERANCE

If the old adage be true—"Discouragement is the best weapon of the Devil,"—then despair must be an indication of surrender to him. And certainly surrender to the power of evil is indication of lack of faith in The Faithful Friend. Do we, or don't we believe his words:

"Let not your hearts be troubled neither let them be afraid." (John 14:27 RSV)

"Whatever you ask in my name, I will do it." (John 14:13 RSV)
"I will not leave you desolate." (John 14:18 RSV)
". . . lo, I am with you always . . ." (Matt. 28:20 RSV)

READ:

        No Room for Discouragement
        Fidelity in Little Things

REVIEW: Page of DISCIPLINES. Are you fulfilling them?

MEDITATE on Scripture: Luke 4: 1-15
                          Romans 7:15 to end of Chapter 8

68

NO ROOM FOR DISCOURAGEMENT *

Jesus Christ has not come to take away all our temptations, nor to eliminate the possibility of sin, rather he has come to take away the sins of the world. The saints themselves were not exempted from the struggle against evil. St. Paul in his Epistle to the Romans underlines this fact: "For I do not understand what I do, for it is not what I wish that I do, but what I hate, that I do . . . For I do not the good that I wish, but the evil that I do not wish, that I perform . . . For I am delighted with the law of God according to the inner man, but I see another law in my members, warring against the law of my mind and making me prisoner to the law of sin that is in my members. Unhappy man that I am: Who will deliver me from the body of this death?"

In the eyes of God, the real value of a man is not to be measured by the ineffectual character of his temptations, or the infrequency of his falls, or even the absence of materially grave sin, but rather first and foremost by his complete confidence in his all-powerful Savior, by his love, and by his determination to keep on trying in spite of failures. As long as traces of discouragement and melancholy persist in your attitude to yourself and your world, you do not yet trust completely in the compassion and forgiveness of the Lord, for the thought of his mercy should fill you with peace and joy.

When the prodigal son returned home, his father wanted nothing more than that the past be forgotten. He ordered a feast so that all might rejoice with him. "There is more joy in heaven over one sinner who repents than over ninety-nine just who have no need of repentance." Jesus Christ hates sin but generously and even lavishly shows pity to the sinner. If you have sinned, the Lord comes to you to show you his love and to offer you his redemptive mercy: the incomprehensible mystery of God's love for men. All things work together unto good for those who love God, even sin. Each fall is a sign, an invitation, to offer yourself to your Savior.

You know your own weakness only too well, you see yourself at the mercy of every onslaught of temptation. Your egocentricity and selfishness seem to be gaining the ascendency rather than decreasing. You are even more acutely aware now of your failure to love. Don't give way to discouragement; rather, rejoice, for the Lord came to save sinners and not the just. If you surrender yourself to him, he will forgive you and lead you to salvation. How can you ask for forgiveness if you do not see the evil which is present in your life?

* Michel Quoist, The Meaning of Success, (c) Copyright: 1963, Fides Publishers, Inc., Reprinted by permission of the copyright holder Fides/Claretian, Notre Dame, Indiana 46556 (pp. 232-235).

NO ROOM FOR DISCOURAGEMENT * (continued)

Why should you come to Jesus Christ in search of salvation if you experience no need for salvation? You will not find peace of mind through greater self-assurance, through a misplaced trust in your own virtue. This kind of peace of mind is pure illusion, for it implies that you no longer have any need of Jesus Christ, and you will find yourself alone, terribly alone and terribly vulnerable, without him. "I have not come to save the just but the sinner." "I have come to save what was lost." "It's not those who are well who have need of the physician but those who are sick."

Be particularly wary of that type of discouragement which can arise out of sins against purity. Sins of this kind can create a feeling of emptiness and malaise which, coupled with a fear of having become the slave of instinct, can lead you to exaggerate your actual situation. Sins of weakness are not to be equated in gravity with sins against faith, hope, and love. A habit of sin restricts the exercise of your freedom, but it also limits your responsibility. If a habit of sin has caught you in its grip, you will have to win back your freedom, but be patient. You shouldn't be discouraged by your own weakness if you recognize at the same time that God's grace is sufficient for you. The grace of God will never fail you but you have to open yourself to receive it. There are two perversions of the Christian moral life which have to be guarded against: staying down once you've fallen and sitting by the side of the road thinking that you've already reached your destination. Your failings should make you recognize your own weakness; they will help you to become a little child again and to place your hand in the Father's as you make your way to your eternal destination.

"I keep the Lord always within my sight; for he is at my right hand, I shall not be moved. For this reason my heart is glad and my soul rejoices; moreover my body also will rest secure." (Psalm 16: 8-9)

Suggested Scriptures for MEDITATION:

    Luke 4: 1-15
    Romans 7:15 to end of Chapter 7
        and all of Chapter 8

---

* Michel Quoist, The Meaning of Success, (c) Copyright: 1963, Fides Publishers, Inc., Reprinted by permission of the copyright holder Fides/Claretian, Notre Dame, Indiana 46556 (pp. 232-235).

FIDELITY IN LITTLE THINGS *

St. Francis de Sales says that great virtues and small fidelities are like salt or sugar. Sugar has a more exquisite taste, but is not used so often. On the contrary, salt enters into all food necessary to life. The great virtues are rare, the occasion for them seldom comes. When it does present itself, we are prepared for it by all that has gone before. We are stirred by the greatness of the sacrifice, we are sustained either by the brilliance of our action in the eyes of others, or by the satisfaction which we have in ourselves in an effort which we find extraordinary. The small occasions are unexpected. They return every moment. They place us constantly at odds with our pride, our idleness, our scorn, our quickness and our chagrin. They come to break our own will in all things, and to leave us no reserve. If we want to be faithful in these small things, nature never has time to breathe, and we must die to all our inclinations. We should a hundred times rather make some great sacrifices to God, however violent and painful, on condition that we be freed with liberty to follow our tastes and habits in every little detail. It is, however, only by faithfulness in little things that the grace of true love sustains us, and distinguishes itself from the passing favours of human nature.

It is with piety as it is with economy in temporal things. If we do not take care of the things near us, we ruin ourselves more in incidental expenses than in great extravagances. Whoever knows how to put the small things to good use, spiritual as well as temporal, accumulates great wealth. All the great things are only made by the accumulation of little things which we receive with care. He who loses nothing will soon grow rich.

Besides, consider that God does not so much seek our deeds, as the motive of love which makes us do them, and the pliancy which he exacts in our will. Men hardly judge our actions except from without. God counts as nothing everything in our actions which seems most brilliant in the eyes of the world. What he wants is a pure intention. It is a will ready for everything, and yielding in his hands. It is a sincere detachment from ourselves. All this is practised more often, with less danger to our pride, and in a way which tests us more sternly, in ordinary occasions rather than in those which are extraordinary. Sometimes even we hold tighter to a trifle than to a great interest. We are more reluctant to give up an amusement than to give away a very large sum. We deceive ourselves the more readily over

---

* François de Salignac de la Mothe Fénelon, Christian Perfection, edited by Charles F. Whiston. Copyright 1947 by Harper & Row, Publishers. Reprinted by permission of the publisher. (pp. 34-36)

FIDELITY IN LITTLE THINGS * (continued)

little things which we think innocent, and to which we think we are less attached. However, when God takes them away, we can easily recognize by the pain of the deprivation how excessive and inexcusable their use and our devotion to them were. Besides, if we neglect the little things, we shock our family all the time, our servants and the whole public. Men cannot think that our piety is in good faith when our behavior seems irregular and weak in detail. How can we make others believe that we should unhesitatingly make the greatest sacrifices, while we fail when it is a question of the smallest ones?

But the most dangerous thing is that the soul, by the neglect of little things, becomes accustomed to unfaithfulness. It saddens Holy Spirit; it yields to its own impulses; it makes nothing of failing God. On the contrary, true love sees nothing as little. Everything which can please or displease God always seems great to it. It is not that true love throws the soul into fussing and scruples, but it does place no limits to its fidelity. It acts simply with God, and as it is quite untroubled by the things which God does not ask of it, it also never wants to hesitate a single instant in that which God does ask of it. Thus, it is not by fussiness that we become faithful and exact in the smallest things. It is by a feeling of love, which is free from the reflections and fears of the anxious and scrupulous. We are as though carried away by the love of God. We only want to do what we are doing, and we do not want to do anything at all which we are not doing. At the same time that God, jealous, urges the soul, presses it relentlessly in the least details, and seems to withdraw all liberty from it, it finds itself free, and it enjoys a profound peace in him. O, how happy it is!

Besides, the people who are naturally more careless of detail are those who should make a stricter law for themselves for the smallest things. We are tempted to be scornful of them. We have a habit of thinking that they do not matter. We do not consider them of enough consequence. We do not realize enough the insensible progress which the passions make; we even forget the most disastrous experiences which we have had with them. We prefer to promise ourselves an imaginary firmness, and to trust to our courage, so many times a deceiver, rather than to bother with a continual faithfulness. "That's nothing," we say. Yes, it is nothing, but a nothing which is all for you; a nothing which you care enough for to refuse it to God; a nothing which

---

* François de Salignac de la Mothe Fénelon, Christian Perfection, edited by Charles F. Whiston. Copyright 1947 by Harper & Row, Publishers. Reprinted by permission of the publisher. (pp. 34-36).

FIDELITY IN LITTLE THINGS * (continued)

you scorn in words so that you may have an excuse to refuse it, but, at bottom, it is a nothing which you are keeping back from God, and which will be your undoing. It is not elevation of the spirit to feel contempt for little things. It is, on the contrary, because of too narrow points of view that we consider as little what has such far-reaching consequences. The more trouble we have to watch ourselves in the little things, the more we must fear to neglect them, the more we must distrust ourselves, and place invincible barriers between ourselves and weakening: Qui spernit modica, paulatim decidet ["He than contemneth small things shall fall by little and little" (Eccles. 19:1)].

In short, judge for yourself. How would you get along with a friend who owed you everything, and who, feeling very much in duty bound to serve you on those rare occasions which we call great, would not take the trouble to show you either kindness or respect in the give and take of ordinary life?

Do not fear this continual attention to little things. At first we must have courage, but this is a penitence which you deserve, which you need, which will make for your peace, and your security. Without it you would have nothing but trouble and relapses. God will give you little by little this sweet and easy state. True love is attentive, without disquiet and without mental conflict.

IN TIME OF TEMPTATION **

Lord and Master, Jesus Christ, who thyself was tempted as we are, yet without sin, give me grace to meet this temptation which now assails me and which I would overcome. Enable me to check all evil thoughts and passions, all enticements to self-indulgence or dishonest gain, and to find, like thee, my highest satisfactions in the doing of my Heavenly Father's will.

---

* François de Salignac de la Mothe Fénelon, Christian Perfection, edited by Charles F. Whiston. Copyright 1947 by Harper & Row, Publishers. Reprinted by permission of the publisher. (pp. 34-36).

** "Prayers for all Occasions," Forward Movement Publications, 412 Sycamore Street, Cincinnati, Ohio 45202. (p. 21)

No. 10 — THANKSGIVING

In Section 8, in the first paragraph of <u>Encounter with God</u>, we read: ". . . like humility, gratitude is the rock bottom foundation for every rule of the spiritual encounter."

As you meditate each day on the daily passages set forth in the next three pages on THANKSGIVING, consider how they apply to your life —and to the life of your faithful friend.

Review the page THE PRACTICE OF THE PRINCIPLES OF FAITH-FUL FRIENDSHIP. Are you forming these habits?

Meditation and Prayer — THANKSGIVING

"Almighty God, Father of all mercies, we, thine unworthy servants, do give thee most humble and hearty thanks for all thy goodness and loving kindness to us, and to all men; we bless thee for our creation, preservation, and all the blessings of this life; but above all, for thine inestimable love in the redemption of the world by our Lord Jesus Christ; for the means of grace, and for the hope of glory. And we beseech thee, give us that due sense of all thy mercies, that our hearts may be unfeignedly thankful; and that we show forth thy praise, not only with our lips, but in our lives, by giving up our selves to thy service, and by walking before thee in holiness and righteous-ness all our days; through Jesus Christ our Lord, to whom, with thee and the Holy Ghost, be all honor and glory, world without end. Amen."

1st day—"For all the blessings of this life"

* "Thankfulness to God for at least some things is an experience which every man has had at some time or other. On recovery from a serious illness, escape from accident, receiving some utterly unex-pected or undeserved fortune; at such moments our hearts are spon-taneously thankful, even though such gratitude may seem at first thought only very dimly related to God. Such experience of thank-fulness is often shallow and temporary, and by no means limited to those who believe in God. But Christian thankfulness is something much deeper than this. Gratitude which is distinctly Christian is not a momentary and surface experience, called forth by some spectacular event in our lives. Rather it is a stable and persistent mood of per-petual thankfulness to God, and is always rooted and grounded in a

---

* Reprinted from <u>Teach Us to Pray</u> by Charles F. Whiston. Copyright, 1949, The Pilgrim Press; coyright renewed, 1977, by Charles F. Whiston.

THANKSGIVING (continued)

deep conviction that the whole of our life is under God's providence
. . . we discover the hidden action of God in the most seemingly trivial
occurrences and circumstances. The practice of the presence of God
opens our eyes to his perpetual presence and action in all that the
whole day and night bring to us.* (p. 136-7)

MEDITATE on "Prayer of General Thanksgiving" on page 73.
PRAY IT.

2nd day—"For all the blessings of this life"

   "When we give thanks, we are to offer them for all the blessings
of this life, in concrete and personal detail . . . Before (God) we are
'children,' with the most elemental needs and the most naive desires
and judgments. To understand this, and to give thanks in the fullest
kind of concreteness, is not childishness but spiritual maturity of the
highest degree. Unless we become as little children, we shall not
enter the kingdom of God—this we have on unimpeachable authority.
(p. 93)

   "To give thanks to God is not to limit our gratitude to ethereal
matters which can be considered properly 'spiritual.' It is, in Evelyn
Underhill's phrase, to 'combine spiritual passion with appreciation of
a cup of coffee'—to love and praise God and to enjoy fully the satisfactions, varieties, and benefits of our earthly life, physical, mental,
emotional, spiritual. (pp. 91-92)

   "To accept the good things of our life in this manner, however,
does not mean that we are to be irresponsible in our use of them, or
free to indulge ourselves for our own gratification and according to
our own desires . . . but (for) such use as may bring us further on
the way to the fulfillment of life which is God's intention in creating
us.** (p. 92)

MEDITATE on the prayer on page 73; then pray your concrete, personal thanks.

---

   * Reprinted from Teach Us to Pray by Charles F. Whiston. Copyright 1949,
The Pilgrim Press; coyright renewed, 1977, by Charles F. Whiston.
** John L. Casteel, Rediscovering Prayer, Copyright 1955, by National Board of
Young Men's Christian Association. Reprinted by permission of Association Press,
Wilton, Conn.

THANKSGIVING (continued)

3rd day—Thankfulness even during adversities

" 'Giving thanks always for all things' was no light and easy affirmation of Paul. This mood of thankfulness to God in all events, even during adversities, is one of the most dominant notes in the letters to Paul. We need here to be most careful to give clear and accurate expression to one of the deepest of Christian convictions. What Paul gave thanks to God for was not the adversities themselves, but for the presence and action and fellowship of God in these adversities. (p. 138-9)

"To give thanks for our troubles, then, is also valid prayer. To do so does not mean that we believe God has deliberately assigned a particular affliction to us. But it is to make an act of faith that when suffering comes, then 'in everything God works for good with those who love him' (Romans 8:28 RSV). When it is not easy to be thankful, as in times of suffering, we can pray for wisdom and strength to accept and use as blessings those circumstances which we are not yet able to receive gratefully. The exhortation of the old hymn is sound Christian practice, even though its motive may appear somewhat naive: 'Count your many blessings, name them one by one; and it will surprise you what the Lord has done . . .' The real outcome of naming our blessings is to grow into the sense of the sacramental meaning of life, in which all the good that comes to us is seen as the gift of God's mercy; and all the suffering as being still within his power to use for our good.* (p. 95-96)

MEDITATE on Romans 8:31-39 and PRAY your prayer of thanksgiving.

4th day—Preparing for abiding thankfulness by daily thankfulness.

". . . we can prepare ourselves, under God, for the coming of deep and abiding Christian thankfulness. We do so by daily giving thanks to God for all that the day has held for us, both of blessings and adversities. Even though at such close range to the actual occurrence we may not yet be able to discern the saving action of God, yet in the light and strength of past experiences of what God has done for us, we confidently meet each trial and vicissitude, knowing that God enters into them to bring us blessing and good, and above all else that during them he gives us his companionship.

Because of this trust and confidence, rooted in past experiences, we daily turn to God at the close of each day and offer him our thankfulness for all that the day has brought to us. Thus we link this prayer of thankfulness closely with our prayer of self-giving, in which

---

* Reprinted from Teach Us to Pray by Charles F. Whiston. Copyright 1949, The Pilgrim Press; copyright renewed, 1977, by Charles F. Whiston.

each night we gather up all that the day has held for us and thankfully place it in the hands of our Father . . . Even when the events of the day go counter to our own will, we turn humbly, trustfully, and thankfully to him and cry our 'Not my will, but thine, be done,' and repeat the prayer:

> Take me from myself, and use me
> As thou wilt,
> Where thou wilt,
> When thou wilt,
> With whom thou wilt.

Slowly over many years of faithful practice of thankfulness, we find that our faith is substantiated by life . . . loss of . . . possessions was necessary and best for us spiritually . . . experiences of temptation and sinning (brought) deeper understanding of ourselves, our weaknesses, . . . our need of God and our need for obedience to him. When our dear ones, still living, go willfully or blindly into the far countries of sin, we give God thanks that not even then does he ever abandon them. Always he accompanies them, seeking to save and redeem them and to turn them back home.* (pp. 140-2)

MEDITATE on Philippians 4:4-9; PRAY your prayer of thankfulness for all that this day has brought to you.

5th day—Watchfulness against Dangers in Prayers of Thanksgiving

* * "In the case of the individual who makes no place in his thought for God (advantages and favorable circumstances often) become the cause of self-congratulation. This is especially the temptation of the 'self-made man.' But the temptation besets others who, in one way or another consent to give God some recognition in their scheme of things. They find their need to give thanks adequately satisfied after the manner of Dorothy Parker's well-to-do Mrs. Whittaker: 'God had always supplied her with the best of service. She could have given Him an excellent reference at any time.' Nor is this kind of acknowledgment restricted to material advantages only. 'God, thank thee that I am not as other men,' prayed the Pharisee, himself a man of no small spiritual attainments, as all might discover who attempted to imitate him in fasting and tithing (Luke 18:11). An individual may

---

* Reprinted from Teach Us to Pray by Charles F. Whiston. Copyright 1949, The Pilgrim Press; copyright renewed, 1977, by Charles F. Whiston.
** John L. Casteel, Rediscovering Prayer. Copyright 1955, by National Board of Young Men's Christian Association. Reprinted by permission of Association Press, Wilton, Conn.

THANKSGIVING (continued)

be moved often to give thanks for what comes to him; but his essential motive in doing so may still be more to congratulate himself and to satisfy his own ego than to acknowledge his dependence upon God and to render him praise.* (p. 87)

MEDITATE on: Luke 15:11-32, especially verse 29; Luke 18:11. PRAY

6th day—"Hope of glory"

"Our hope of glory is God and our sense of the eternal life is the consciousness of being in communion with him. Not the aura of a person absent, but the overpowering recognition of a Person present, leads us to rejoice and give him thanks . . . Our prayers of thanksgiving . . . will go beyond the act of naming and being grateful for the concrete circumstances of life, and will find occasion for us to pour out in praise our love for God.* (p. 99)

MEDITATE on: John 14:1-3, 16-17, and 25-27. PRAY, thankfully.

7th day—"Show forth thy praise"

"When we have given thanks to God for all the blessings of this life and for the redemption of this life into one filled with the 'hope of glory,' the prayer of general thanksgiving carries us back into the living of life itself . . . that 'we may show forth thy praise in our lives, by giving up our selves to thy service, and by walking before thee in holiness and righteousness all our days.' Once more, the practice of praying becomes the life of prayer . . . we rise to the level of life where persons count more than things, where the relations of personal love displace posessiveness and self-gratification, where what vitally matters is that we shall love God and shall be held by his love for us. To give thanks, then, is to accept the life God has given us joyfully and confidently, and to answer his lovingkindness with our own offering of that life back to him. 'O give thanks unto the Lord, for he is good; his mercy endureth forever.' * (pp. 100-1, 102).

MEDITATE on any one of these psalms: 30, 35, 27, 103, 104, 107, 116. Pray your own prayer of thankfulness and self-offering.

"I give Thee back the life I owe—that in Thine ocean depths its flow may richer, fuller be."

---

* John L. Casteel, Rediscovering Prayer. Copyright 1955, by National Board of Young Men's Christian Association. Reprinted by permission of Association Press, Wilton. Conn.

THANKSGIVING (continued)

PRAYER OF THANKSGIVING *

"For all the things for which we have never given thanks to thee, O Lord, we humbly bow our hearts. For common things of earth which sustain our bodies in health and strength, though we pay scant attention to them, we give thanks. For far-off things in the ages past or in lands distant from us which enlarge our heritage and expand our horizon, we give thee thanks. For invisible things of heaven and earth which sweeten life with beauty and grace, we give thee thanks. For things of the spirit which disclose to us the beauty of thy holiness and sanctify the passing of time with eternal meaning, we give thee thanks. For things bought with a great price, given to us without cost, by which we are deepened and heightened to the measure of Christ our Lord, we give thee thanks. Though there be no end to thy gifts, help us to number them as they are revealed to us day by day. Amen."

---

* Samuel H. Miller, Prayers for Daily Use. Copyright (c) 1957 by Samuel H. Miller. Reprinted by permission of Harper & Row, Publishers, Inc. (pp. 119-120).

No. 11 — SPIRITUAL DIRECTION
THROUGH FAITHFUL FRIENDSHIP

PERUSE the pages "Spiritual Direction through Faithful Friendship."

CONSIDER each paragraph.

What have you discovered in these weeks of praying for, praying with, and studying with another whom you have called 'faithful friend'?

Do you keep reminding each other that each of you has, and together you have The Faithful Friend ever present, ever encouraging, ever inspiring and strengthening you?

What have you learned, and what can you learn from these paragraphs about spiritual direction?

Suggested Scripture for MEDITATION:
Isaiah 9:6
John 14—especially vs. 16 and 26
Matthew 18:20
John 15:12-17

REVIEW the page: "A Close Look at Faithful Friendship." (Section No. 2).

SPIRITUAL DIRECTION THROUGH FAITHFUL FRIENDSHIP

Any two persons who adopt the disciplines and earnestly practice the principles of faithful friendship will ever remember and remind one another of the constant presence of their Faithful Friend—the Spirit of Jesus Christ, the Holy Spirit, the Wonderful Counselor. As the two friends endeavor to grow in the life of the spirit and in knowledge and love of one another, the Wonderful Counselor imbues them with a degree of wisdom, prudence and discernment that enables them to be helpful encouragers and guides of each other.

The following excerpts from Merton's little book, Spiritual Direction,* will help faithful friends to understand what the Wonderful Counselor has in mind for them as together they prepare to serve him by receiving from him—and giving for, by, and through him—some degree of spiritual direction.

God is going to get his work done if he is taken seriously. (Coburn).

". . . the director is not to be regarded as a magical machine for solving cases and declaring the holy will of God beyond all hope of appeal, but a trusted friend who, in an atmosphere of sympathetic understanding, helps and strengthens us in our groping efforts to correspond with the grace of the Holy Spirit, who alone is the true Director in the fullest sense of the word. (preface)

". . . we can best profit by spiritual direction if we are encouraged to develop our natural simplicity, sincerity, and forthright spiritual honesty, in a word to 'be ourselves' in the best sense of the expression. (preface)

"Spiritual direction is not merely the cumulative effect of encouragements and admonitions which we all need in order to live up to our state in life. It is not mere ethical, social or psychological guidance. It is spiritual. (p. 6)

"The spiritual man is one who, 'whether he eats or drinks or whatever else he does, does all for the glory of God' (I Cor. 10:31). Again, this does not mean that he merely registers in his mind an abstract intention to glorify God. It means that in all his actions he is free from the superficial automatism of conventional routine. It means that in all that he does he acts freely, simply, spontaneously, from the depths of his heart, moved by love.* (p. 7)

---

* Thomas Merton, Spiritual Direction and Meditation. Published by The Liturgical Press, 1960. Copyrighted by The Order of St. Benedict, Inc., Collegeville, Minnesota.

SPIRITUAL DIRECTION THROUGH FAITHFUL FRIENDSHIP (cont.)

"Direction . . . speaks to the whole man, in the concrete circumstances of his life, however simple they may be. (p. 8)

"The first thing that genuine spiritual direction requires in order to work properly is a normal, spontaneous human relationship. (p. 11)

"What we need to do is bring the director into contact with our real self, as best we can, and not fear to let him see what is false in our false self. Now this right away implies a relaxed, humble attitude in which we let go of ourselves and renounce our unconscious efforts to maintain a façade. We must let the director know what we really think, what we really feel, and what we really desire, even when these things are not altogether honorable. We must be quite frank about our motives insofar as we can be so. The mere effort to admit that we are not as unselfish or as zealous as we pretend to be is a great source of grace. (pp. 24-25)

"It is . . . respect for the mystery of personality that makes a real director: this, together with common sense, the gift of prayer, patience, experience, and sympathy. (p. 26)

"True simplicity implies love and trust—it does not expect to be derided and rejected, any more than it expects to be admired and praised. It simply hopes to be accepted on its own terms. This is the kind of atmosphere which a good director tries to produce: an atmosphere of confidence and friendliness in which the penitent can say anything that is on his mind with the assurance that it will be dealt with frankly and honestly. (pp. 29-30)

"The director wants to know our inmost self, our real self . . . He wants to know the inmost truth of our vocation, the action of grace in our souls. His direction is, in reality, nothing more than a way of leading us to see and obey our real Director—the Holy Spirit, hidden in the depths of our soul. We must never forget that in reality we are not directed and taught by men, and that if we need human 'direction' it is only because we cannot, without man's help, come into contact with that 'unction (of the Spirit) which teaches us all things.' (I John 2:20) (p. 30)

"In oral spiritual direction, much is communicated without words, even in spite of words. The direct person-to-person relationship is something that cannot be adequately replaced. Christ Himself said, 'Where two or three are gathered together in My Name, there am I in the midst of them.' There is a special spiritual presence of Christ in direct personal conversation, which guarantees a deeper and more intimate expression of the whole truth.* (p. 39)

---

* Thomas Merton, Spiritual Direction and Meditation. Published by The Liturgical Press, 1960. Copyrighted by The Order of St. Benedict, Inc., Collegeville, Minnesota.

No. 12—LOOKING BACK AT YOUR DIRECTION IN ORDER TO LOOK AHEAD AT YOUR SPIRITUAL DIRECTION

Having had a faithful friend, you have experienced being listened to,

    accepted
        loved
            confronted
                forgiven
                    supported.

Having been a faithful friend, you have listened to another,

    accepted
        loved
            confronted
                forgiven
                    supported your friend.

You and your faithful friend have been enabled, through the power at work within you both, to accomplish far more abundantly than you could ask or think.

You have been stretching, growing, increasing in the capacity to relate affirmatively to all your associates. You are becoming more and more nearly that person you are intended to be.

You are actively participating in The Great Enterprise. . . .
    you are obeying the New Covenant—
        increasing in love of God and love of neighbor.

READ and absorb the following pages . . . and MEDITATE on the final page together with the Scripture suggested.

THE MOUNT OF PURIFICATION *

We are none of us quite the same as this time last year are we? If we were asked why, we would say, "Oh! So much has happened!" It is God's action that has happened: His action through events on us, and our response or lack of response. His hand held the hammer and chisel, the scrubbing-brush and the polishing rag of circumstance, which we either endured or dodged.

So let us begin our self-examination by looking back at the past year from that point of view. What tests did He administer to our courage and our trust? What openings for generosity, self-denial, forgiveness? What events have tested our supposed good qualities and showed up their weakness under strain? What sudden joys gave a chance for gratitude? What things or people humbled us? What disappointments and sorrows gave us a chance to practice the resignation we always talk about, and what annoyances braced our self-control? Look at them! Every one of them are graces, "touches of God" as the mystics say, chances of growing a bit in the Christian life. Did we take them? Or waste them? . . ." The whole wisdom of the Saints," says St. John of the Cross, "consists in directing the will vigorously towards God": and the way that is done by ordinary people like ourselves is by aiming at Him in all the circumstances of life.

What matters supremely to our soul's growth is how we lay hold on life: whether we let it just go on without giving it significance, or whether we so respond to the mesh of circumstance that through and in it we find God. Our job, our environment, however narrow, is always adequate to this, because there is no place or circumstance where God is not.

It is consoling to remember that circumstances can do nothing to us, to our deepest selves, because they can neither help nor hinder, save in so far as we do or do not direct our will through them to God. We are not required to adjust ourselves to circumstances by some awful wrench; but to let circumstances be, let them happen, be quiet in them and do our best without fuss; and then God will come to us in them, however hostile to our own notion of spiritual life, peace and happiness, they may be. For instance, ill health or unexpected stress and duties have made our rule of life, our most cherished practice, impossible. Well! God is not in the practice, not even the most holy practice. That may have seemed your path but in His richness and freedom, He has an infinity of paths. The changes and chances of life have given you Martha's job when you felt called to that of Mary;

* Evelyn Underhill, The Mount of Purification, Copyright Longmans, Green & Co. 1960.

THE MOUNT OF PURIFICATION * (continued)

if it was a real call, it transcends circumstances: you will still find the one thing needful among the pots and pans. It would not have helped the growth of Martha's soul if she had sat down with Mary and, as a very pious cook once said when she wished to go to church, "Let the Holy Ghost see to the breakfast." Martha was a domestic soul and could have found God fully among domestic things, if she had taken them the right way. It was not her usefulness, it was her spirit of fuss that spoilt her capacity for Him. She was so full up with jobs, plans, worries, things that must be done, that she had ceased to direct her will vigorously towards Reality; she had lost her sense of proportion and was swamped by the mere flood of that use and wont which might have conveyed Reality to her.

Have we all got Martha-ish in a bad sense? And have we got the notion that the right way to cure it is to chuck our job and take Mary's in its place? Because it does not at all follow that that is so. The real remedy for the spirit of fuss lies much deeper than that. It lies, as Dante saw when he wrote the Purgatorio, in a stern and faithful setting-in-order of our love, getting the proportion of existence right. In modern jargon, get your scale of values right and whatever the job you are called to, it will help your soul to grow towards God.

Those who read Dante will remember what a wonderful picture there is in the Purgatorio of that gradual cleansing of the soul from its natural selfishness and unreality, by the Fire and Light of God's love, the preparing of it for a life of perfect love. Now that cleansing process forms a large part of our spiritual life, and it can, if we choose, be done to us through circumstances, here and now. It is our own fault, says Friedrich von Hugel, if we do not get purified in this life.

And one principle runs through it all, a principle we shall do well to get fixed in our heart's depth. It is not our normal life, feelings, passions, the drive of our God-given nature—a nature shared by Christ Himself—which is hostile to our spiritual life, but simply the direction we give it or let it take. It is true we are fitted with an explosive sort of engine, but we need not let it backfire. Sin is the self-regarding, irresponsible use of instinct, which cripples the will, the real driving-force of the soul, which is always, when pure, tending to move towards God —the supreme attraction, the supreme life. Sin is the downward drag of our energetic nature turned the wrong way and that can only be cured by turning it the right way, using its energy for God, and not merely squashing it down.

* Evelyn Underhill, The Mount of Purification, Copyright Longmans, Green & Co. 1960.

THE MOUNT OF PURIFICATION * (continued)

Here psychology and religion go hand in hand and spiritual right-
ness—setting love in order, cleansing our desire and intention from
the stain of self that we may be what God wishes us to be and so
enter into His Joy—is the central thought to keep before us. And we
will take Dante's journey up the purifying mountain as a map on which
to find our own way. We all know the general scheme of that wonderful journey—how he clambered up from terrace to terrace, not
forced by God's justice but drawn by His love and by his own passion-
ate longing to correspond with that love. And on each terrace one
of the great perversions of human instinct is painfully and faithfully
put right. Put right because the soul sees not so much its own horrid-
ness as the opposite virtue shining in celestial beauty and loves it so
much, that no price is too high to pay. The bliss and beauty of the
meek, merciful, peaceful, pure; the bit by bit realization of the rich
wonder of Holiness as that for which our souls are really made. That
is ever so much more illuminating and humiliating than counting
our own spots and makes us much more ashamed.

On each terrace we are shown an example from the life of the
Blessed Virgin Mary—her humility over against our folly of pride:
her gentleness over our tendency to uproar and anger: her generosity
over against our inveterate grab: her purity over against all excess of
desire. Why? Because Mary stands for simple human nature as it
ought to be—a pure capacity for God: full of grace because emptied
of self; and so she is the classical pattern of every human soul
turned to Him, whether the special vocation of that soul is prayer
or service—homely, quiet self-sacrifice or great initiative. In all this,
what matters is simply our capacity for God and our self-oblivious
response. The true work of prayer, self-conquest, suffering, is to increase our latent capacity for God and so make us more useful to
Him. Behold the handmaid of the Lord: be it unto me according to
Thy word: body and soul at the disposal of the Spirit.

The awful gap we are conscious of in ourselves between the I of
the surface life, self-interested, swayed by instinct, unrestful, easily
upset—and the ME, the deep soul we humbly trust is our true self,
did not exist in Mary. We have to bridge this gap by the gradual
growth of the ME and the conquest of the I: and to do this is the very
essence of a real life of prayer. For the life of the ME, the soul's
ground, is a prayer: its existence is a correspondence with God: all
its experiences are related to God and its aspiration is "Be it unto me
according to Thy word." But the I lives on the surface: all its experiences are related to its own needs and instincts; it wishes to express
itself, develop itself, and all that.

---

* Evelyn Underhill, The Mount of Purification, Copyright Longmans, Green & Co.
1960.

THE MOUNT OF PURIFICATION * (continued)

A full-grown spiritual life is one in which God holds His undivided sway; not only over the ME, which we call the spiritual side of our nature: but over the I, that is both over the surface and over the deeps. God desires to transform us, to remake us in His order, the order of the Holy: and those who have the nerve to accept that destiny with all its costs, can become part of the mystical Body through which His Spirit acts on life. Be ye holy as I am—holy! Look at that! Look, so far as we may, at the purity, power, beauty and generosity of God, revealed in Christ; then look at the twisted, tangled and conflicting desires of our own nature, all its frittered energies. The Mount of Purification does not seem too big, does it? for all the distance to be travelled and all the work that has got to be done—twisting back into the right line our perverted desire; moderating; tempering its excesses, bracing up our insufficient zest; cleaning and reordering the primitive and instinctive layers of our half-made human nature, and weaving them up into the personality that shall serve the purpose of God and be a sacrament of His communion with men. Those primitive dispositions and selfish instincts with their pulls and pushes are in all of us, either in crude or subtle form.

The form of sin may be different in us but the substance is the same—self-love, self-interest, self-will. The thrusting energy and instinct of our nature has not changed since the thirteenth century (when Dante lived and wrote) and those instincts must all be trained away from self and on to God if our love is to fulfill itself. And we can do it here in this life, this vale of soul-making, if we choose. The mountain stands before us now. Sooner or later we have got to climb it. That is involved in choosing Christ. The moment we start, God's cooperation will also start, for starting means yielding ourselves to Him and we have got to do it now. The substance of this present life is, every bit of it, part of the scenery of that Mount of Purification and the nature with which we emerge from infancy is the material we are to purify and consecrate to God.

And so as we think of the re-ordering of our character, the releasing and purifying of our love in its double aspect, first self-conquest, the struggle up the mountain, and second, the passive mortification and grateful acceptance of all God deigns to do to us there, we will also keep in mind and direct our prayers to a third fact, the goal, the positive quality of a life transformed in God: we will keep on looking at the summit, however hot and breathless and "fed-up" we may get from time to time.

---

* Evelyn Underhill, The Mount of Purification, Copyright Longmans, Green & Co. 1960.

THE MOUNT OF PURIFICATION * (continued)

It may seem a long way off, but there it is in its reality and beauty: giving something of its own wonder and beauty to the long slogging ascent which always forms the main part of a real climb. With one eye we will look on process and with one eye we will look on the End. God's perfection, already fully present, is ready to enfold us, give us of His very life as soon as we can take it in.

In our whole life of prayer and speculation . . . we need to keep both eyes in focus. And that does not mean a spiritual squint, for the process and the end are both enclosed in God and lead to God. And at last we see they are two sides of one life in which all our activities become ever more and more the expression of His deep creative action and all our efforts are penetrated by His unchanging Peace.

(Portions of pp. 7 to 13 and 17-18.)

---

* Evelyn Underhill, The Mount of Purification, Copyright Longmans, Green & Co. 1960.

FRIENDSHIPS IN THE FUTURE *

John Barth has captured the sense of turnover among friendships in a passage from his novel The Floating Opera: "Our friends float past; we become involved with them; they float on, and we must rely on hearsay or lose track of them completely; they float back again, and we must either renew our friendship—catch up to date— or find that they and we don't comprehend each other any more." The only fault in this is its unspoken suggestion that the current upon which friendships bob and float is lazy and meandering. The current today is picking up speed. Friendship increasingly resembles a canoe shooting the rapids of the river of change. "Pretty soon," says Professor Eli Ginzberg of Columbia University, an expert on manpower mobility, "we are all going to be metropolitan-type people in this country without ties or commitments to long-time friends and neighbors."

In a brilliant paper on "Friendships in the Future," psychologist Courtney Tall suggests that "Stability based on close relationships with a few people will be ineffective, due to the high mobility, wide interest range, and varying capacity for adaptation and change found among the members of a highly automated society . . . Individuals will develop the ability to form close 'buddy-type' relationships on the basis of common interests or sub-group affiliations, and to easily leave these friendships, moving either to another location and joining a similar interest group or to another interest group within the same location. Interests will change rapidly . . ."

This ability to form and then to drop, or lower to the level of acquaintanceship, close relations quickly, coupled with increased mobility, will result in any given individual forming many more friendships than is possible for most in the present . . . Friendship patterns of the majority in the future will provide for many satisfactions, while substituting many close relationships of shorter durability for the few long-term friendships formed in the past.

---

* Alvin Toffler, Future Shock. Copyright 1970, Alvin Toffler. Reprinted by permission of Random House, Inc. (Portions of pp. 93, 94, and 106)

FRIENDSHIPS IN THE FUTURE * (continued)

How fast should (persons) be expected to make and break human relationships? Perhaps there is some optimum rate that we exceed at our peril? Nobody knows. However, if to this picture of declining durations we add the factor of diversity—the recognition that each new human relationship requires a different pattern of behavior from us—one thing becomes starkly clear: to be able to make these increasingly numerous and rapid on-off clicks in our interpersonal lives we must be able to operate at a level of adaptability never before asked of human beings.

Until now most of us have operated on the assumption that temporary relationships are superficial relationships, that only long-enduring ties can flower into real interpersonal involvement. Perhaps this assumption is false. Perhaps it is possible for holistic, non-modular relationships, to flower rapidly in a high transcience society. It may prove possible to accelerate the formation of relationships, and to speed up the process of "involvement" as well.

. . . with respect to all three of the tangible components of situations—people, places and things—the rate of turnover is rising. It is time now to look at those intangibles that are equally important in shaping experience, the information we use and the organizational frameworks within which we live.

SCRIPTURE FOR MEDITATION

"Put out into the deep and let down your nets for a catch."
(Luke 5:4 RSV)

The command: "Put out into deep water . . ." (Luke 5:4 Jer.)

Obedience: "But if you say so . . ." (Luke 5:6 Jer.)

The assurance: "Do not be afraid; henceforth you will be catching men." (Luke 5:14 RSV)

"What is the secret of your life?" asked Mrs. Browning of Charles Kingsley. "Tell me, that I may make mine beautiful, too." He replied, "I had a friend."

---

* Alvin Toffler, Future Shock. Copyright 1970, Alvin Toffler. Reprinted by permission of Random House, Inc. (Portions of pp. 93, 94, and 106)

AN OPEN LETTER TO FAITHFUL FRIENDS

Not until the manuscript for this handbook was ready for the printer did Aelred's little book, Spiritual Friendship [1], fall into my hands. I read it with mounting exhilaration, having first learned of it through William Johnston's Silent Music [2]. Aelred describes the highest reaches of genuine spiritual friendship. Unfortunately, few there be who scale those heights. No cause, however, for discouragement; rather, it is stimulating to read of the possibility. We keep our eye on that possibility as Christian in Pilgrim's Progress was advised by Evangelist to keep his eye on the Light in order to pass through the wicket gate.

You and your faithful friend have glimpsed the joy and strength to be derived from a relationship fostered and developed under the guidance of the ever-present Christ. As you now seek further to deepen your relationship with Jesus Christ and your faithful friend —continuing the disciplines, practicing the principles of faithful friendship, making your own selections of Scripture for daily meditation and your own selections of collateral reading—remember that through the power at work within you he is "able to do far more abundantly" than all you can ask or think.

My faithful friend and I have prepared and had printed this small book believing we are dropping in a pond a pebble that can cause ever-widening ripples; and that, if it be God's will, the ripples could even become, in this sadly strife-torn world, a tidal wave of goodwill among men.

Can you envision ways of using your gifts and the gifts of your friend in order to "put out into the deep"—and to "go and make disciples"—by being a friend because He sends you as He was sent by the Father? Remember He said. ". . . he who believes in me will also do the works that I do; and greater works than these will he do, because I go to the Father" (John 14:12 RSV).

If you have any questions about continuing structure or study materials—or if you have helpful suggestions for us—communication from you to Mimi or to me would be warmly welcomed.

Faithfully,

Dorothy C. Devers
309 Yoakum Parkway Apt. 603
Alexandria, Va. 22304

Mimi C. Spillers
205 Yoakum Parkway
Alexandria, Va. 22304

March 1979

---

[1] Aelred of Rievaulx, Spiritual Friendship, Cistercian Publications, Kalamazoo, Michigan, 1977.
[2] William Johnston, Silent Music, Cy 1974 William Johnston, Harper & Row, Publishers.

Cover Design by Joan McGuire